And Babies Make

Seven

By: V. J. Koning Keelan

AND BABIES MAKE SEVEN

Published by Septimal Publishing

Septimalpublishing.ca

ISBN-13:
978-0-9811795-0-6

Cover art by: Beeline
First edition: May 2009

Chapter	Page

List of Illustrations

Acknowledgement:

"You should write a book…" It was a common response when I told someone what one of the kids had done, or how Bryan and I had coped with yet another stressful incident concerning our family.

I had already written my memories of the car accident I was in, which had been published in an Anglican Church magazine in 1974. It seemed a logical next step to expand the story from just my life and include my marriage and add Bryan's early years as well. However, it wasn't until I met with Margaret, my mentor, in 2005, that my writing started to have purpose. It was she who encouraged me to get serious about writing a book.

My husband kept a diary during the long weeks that we were separated in 1985. Using it, I was able to write about my hospital stay in Women's College Hospital. Without it, part of my story would be lost. My memory of those weeks is quite fuzzy.

My mother kept all the letters I wrote to her, detailing the minutiae of our life in the 1990's. ("Only a mother would be interested in hearing this drivel," I thought as I mailed my letters.) But my father was in the hospital, unable to speak because of a stroke, and I knew Mom appreciated having something to read to him. Those letters supplied much of the material later in the book.

My son, Geoffrey, read through several versions of the manuscript and made many helpful suggestions. My daughter, Meghan, was another reader, making suggestions and prodding my memory. My sister-in-law Rosemary read several versions as well, at my insistence. There are many people in Peterborough and beyond, thanks to email, who endured my endless "Do you remember…" ramblings and who answered questions about babies and young children. Others provided editorial help at various stages in the writing process.

Thank you to all who supported me in this project.

But it is my family, Bryan, Meghan, Geoffrey, Alan, Richard and Paul who deserve most of the credit; otherwise there would be no reason for a book.

Valerie

Peterborough, 2009

Prologue

Stillness...darkness...then metal shrieking on metal. A farmer runs out of his barn, pauses, and races to the house. He opens the front door and yells: "Thelma! Sounds like a car crash. Call the cops. I'm going to see if I can help."

He jumps into his truck and starts to drive, checking the glove compartment for the first aid kit. When he reaches the crash site, he stops and climbs out of the truck.

"Dear Lord," he breathes. He isn't a religious man, but he crosses himself as he surveys two mangled masses of metal, bodies flung from one and jumbled in the other.

        *   *   *

The knocking on the door was insistent, and Jean had a faint sense of unease as she walked down the hall. Visitors at this time of night usually meant bad news.

"Tell Father he's got to come...quick. A terrible accident. The Orange Hall. Oh my god, they're all dead..."

He turned quickly and left.

"Tony-" Jean started to call her husband, the Anglican priest in this small village on the Manitoulin Island.

"I heard," he said, turning off the TV. "We'd better take the car."

1

Prologue

He pulled his overcoat tighter as he walked down the porch steps. It was the end of March, but light snow had fallen that day. He brushed it off the car with his glove.

Jean grabbed her coat and a prayer book and followed him out. Neither spoke for the five minute trip. Tony pulled into the Dairy Queen parking lot opposite the Hall. After getting out of the car, they crossed the street. Several people were huddled together, smoking, with their heads down. Jean's inner antennae sparked and she felt a prickling sensation at the back of her neck.

Inside the hall they stopped. Lying in front of the stage were four blanket-wrapped figures. A murmur of men's voices…a bump of someone passing them. They had to step to one side for two men carrying yet another heavy bundle of blankets.

A woman rushed over and grabbed Tony's arm.

"Father, come here."

As they moved away, Jean cautiously approached the bodies lying on the floor. Another had come in, making a total of six and still more were coming. She wrinkled her nose at the wet blanket smell and then she noticed that one face was slightly visible.

"My God," she thought, bending over to look. "That's Terry."

Her eyes scanned the other bundles. Please, God, no! Where was her daughter? Across the room she spotted an OPP officer. She went to him and grabbed his sleeve. "Mike, Val was with them! Where is she?"

The officer turned to look at her. He touched her arm briefly.

"Wait here." He conferred with another officer and returned. "Val's in Little Current."

"Thank heavens," she thought. Then she looked in his eyes. Her stomach clenched.

"She was badly injured and has been taken to the hospital," he said. "I'm sorry, Jean."

She turned and stumbled to her husband, talking quietly to a crying woman.

"Val's in Little Current, at the hospital. We have to go."

In the car, Jean glanced at Tony, but didn't mention the speed. Surely God would keep them safe. They had to get to the hospital.

"Oh God, Tony. What if she dies before we get there?" Jean cried.

"Don't say that," her husband commanded. "We don't know…" He couldn't continue.

Twenty minutes later Tony parked at the hospital. They pushed through the doors, into a scene of calm chaos. Several nurses were moving swiftly, tending bodies on stretchers.

A gurney by itself…a body with long blond hair spread out to one side. Val! Her eyes were closed, but her chest rose and fell rhythmically. She was alive!

"Jean, Tony." The doctor shook each of their hands in turn. "Val's unconscious and we can't deal with her injuries here. I'm sending her to a hospital in the city."

They followed the ambulance, the two vehicles driving cautiously. The twisting, winding road eventually joined the main highway. As the driving became easier, both vehicles picked up speed.

"We have to believe…We have to have faith…." Tony attempted conversation, but seemed unable to form a thought.

Jean sat with her face turned to the window. She didn't notice the craggy rocks and trees, scenery she'd marvelled at on other trips. She didn't see the wooden houses, restaurants, and gas bars as they sped through towns. Her mind wandered back over the past four hours. What could she have done differently? What *should* she have done differently? If only…she'd told her daughter she couldn't go. If only…she'd listened to Tony. If only…but nothing could change what had happened.

"Our Father, who art in heaven…" Jean began reciting the familiar words out loud and Tony joined in. "Thy will be done, on earth as it is in heaven…" They finished the prayer in unison and fell silent. As more miles passed, Jean silently read the Evening Prayer service.

At the hospital the ambulance went one way and Tony the other, to the parking lot. Inside, the anxious couple had to sit in the waiting room while the doctor made his initial examination. He looked solemn as he approached them.

"George Walker." He said as he extended his hand.

They each shook it in turn, and both spoke at once, "How is she? Is she going to live?"

"She's had massive head trauma and we won't know what that means for a while. Also, both her femurs are broken." He touched his thigh to indicate which bone it was. "We'll put her legs in traction. I'd rather not operate while she's in a coma."

"Can we see her?" they asked.

"Follow me," the doctor said, turning to leave.

Tony motioned for Jean to go first as they followed the doctor to the ICU, the intensive care unit. They entered the room and saw a nurse sitting with their daughter, lying still with an intravenous line connected to her hand. Her father made the sign of the cross on her forehead, giving her a blessing.

*　　　　*　　　　*

And Babies Make Seven

May, 1970:

My brother and I are at the hospital. We climb into an ambulance. Then...there's a lady lying on a stretcher beside me. She tells me to go to sleep, as she has done. The driver turns around and glares at me. He speeds up and drives off the road. We're in a field of sweet smelling flowers. It is very peaceful. Then...white walls and a white ceiling. I'm lying flat on my back, rolling along. Then...I'm in a wheelchair. Through an open door I can see the car. Please! Let me go to it! If I could feel the soft coolness of the black leather, the back seat, against my cheek, I would wake up. This is a really bad dream. Unless...it isn't a dream...

God grant me the serenity to accept the things I cannot change, courage to change the things I can, and the wisdom to know the difference.

I have to get out of these ropes. After twisting and turning, pulling and pushing, I'm free. I sit on the edge of the bed and start to stand. I hear rather than feel my head hitting the floor. Then, soothing hands comfort me. I'm in ropes again, and I wiggle to get out. When I'm tangled, I stop moving. I won't choke; soothing hands will comfort me.

Where am I? Am I dead? I don't think so. What if no one knows I'm here? What if they think I'm dead? What if they try to bury me? But I don't think I'm dead! I have to tell Mom. Don't let them bury me. I'm not dead. I have to tell her. Don't let them bury me. I'm not dead.

"Mom, Mom, Mom, Mom, Mom, Mom..."

The words seemed to be coming from their daughter's room as Jean and Tony walked past the nurse's station. They looked at the nurse who smiled as she nodded her head.

"She's awake?" Jean asked.

"She just started talking. But she might not be responsive yet."

5

Prologue

They rushed into their daughter's room, anxious to see for themselves that she was waking up. But she was lying silently.

Over the next twenty-four hours their daughter seemed to waken occasionally and tried to talk. Jean put her ear near Val's mouth but her whisper was inaudible. Other times she lay still, as if asleep.

In an effort to stimulate communication, Jean brought a chalkboard to the hospital. During her daughter's wakeful periods, Jean put her in a sitting position and put the board within reach. She offered her daughter a piece of chalk and although she was right-handed, Val took it in her left hand. The right side of her body was immobile. She scribbled, "I can walk. The doctor says I can go home."

She seemed to know she'd been injured, and that she was in a hospital. What else did she know?

Two days later, Val whispered and Jean heard: "Mom...ask... Paul...to...come...visit...me."

She obviously had no memory of the car accident. Jean stroked her daughter's face, pushing her hair off her forehead. As hard as it was to speak of the tragedy, it was her duty as a mother to relate the news.

"Oh Val, I hate to have to tell you this, but Paul was killed in the car accident you were in."

Val was silent. Finally, in her peculiar flat voice, she said, "Was...anyone...else...killed."

Jean stroked the back of Val's hand, tears streaming down her face.

"Yes. Ann, Boyne, Hugh, Terry, and Wayne. Marty was in the car, and was injured, but he's alive. Three people died in the other car, but you didn't know them."

Val looked at her mother, her face blank.

1: There Are How Many?

"Mummy, Daddy, open the door. Come and get me."

My two-year-old daughter, Meghan, chanted her mantra as I lay in bed, listening. My husband, Bryan, shifted beside me.

We'd agreed when we'd made the decision to start a family that I would be the main caregiver during the early years. Because of my inability to run, Bryan would assume chasing duties as our daughter grew. I rolled out of bed and shuffled down the hall. As I pushed the door and looked in the room, I smiled.

My daughter was sitting in the middle of her bed, her arms outstretched. With her strawberry blond hair reaching almost to her ears, she resembled me at that age. My hair had darkened over time and now matched my brown eyes. Meggie's eyes were hazel like her Dad's. I sat on the bed and took her onto my lap.

"Good morning, Meggie." I hugged her and kissed her cheek, delighting in holding her. That I'd been able to give birth, after the injuries I'd received, always amazed me.

"Morning Mummy," she said, reaching to put her arms around my neck. I felt the soft coolness of her cheek against mine. She smelled sweet.

I preferred to sit while embracing her because of my poor balance. Carrying her as a baby, she'd fit in one arm, leaving the other free to steady myself as needed. But as she grew, lugging her around had become increasingly difficult. Luckily for me, Meggie learned to walk at an early age.

There Are How many?

I held her hand as we went into the bathroom next to her bedroom. As we walked back into the hall, I said, "Let's go to my bedroom, okay? Mummy and Daddy want to sleep for a while longer."

"Okay. Daddy sleep?"

"Yes, Daddy and I want to sleep."

We walked together into the bedroom, and letting go of her hand, I climbed into bed, in hopes of recapturing the warm cosiness. Meggie ran around to the other side of the bed. Her feet, clad in a sleeper, made whooshing sounds on the carpet.

She took Bryan's glasses off his bedside table, and standing beside the bed, sang "Da-dee, Da-dee, Da-dee," rocking side to side until, without opening his eyes, he stuck his hand out from under the blankets. She deposited the glasses in it, and satisfied that she'd performed her task, walked back to my side of the bed.

"Daddy have g'asses, Mum," she announced as she climbed onto the bed and sat between us. By this time Bryan and I were laughing. As our daughter settled herself atop the blankets, my husband started tickling her. There would be no more sleep now.

My name is Valerie Koning. Or that's what it was in 1985, when this part of my story began. I had kept my maiden name when I married, but in the early 1990's, I added my husband's name, Keelan.

I lived in a small city in Southern Ontario, Canada, with my husband and daughter. We had two cats and considered ourselves an ordinary, one-income family. Bryan earned a wage, but I was unable to work outside the house due to my physical limitations.

There were certain things I couldn't do as a result of injuries sustained in a car accident fifteen years previously. That monumental event might've been enough for one lifetime, but fate had intervened. It started with our desire to have a family.

Two years after our marriage we began to think about having children, but we hadn't known how I'd cope with being pregnant. A woman's body changes during pregnancy and her sense of balance compensates. My equilibrium had been affected by my brain injury.

As my pregnancy progressed, however, I'd only had to quit riding my bicycle. My gait, a little wobbly at times, remained unchanged. I'd been living with it for a decade and considered it normal.

It was time to get up. Bryan carried Meggie downstairs, letting me go first to put the kettle on for his coffee and my tea. In the kitchen, he pulled a chair out to sit at the table, and put his daughter on his knee.

As I watched them playing peek-a-boo, I reflected on what Meggie's birth had taught me about love. There are different forms of that emotion, but for me, loving my daughter and feeling protective of her, was an entirely new sensation.

Since 1970, I'd always been on the receiving end of such sentiments. My parents and brothers and later my husband had guided me, offering an arm as I walked down stairs, or in crowds. I had accepted the assistance in the spirit it was offered, rarely spurning offers of help. It was a beneficial trait, I was to discover.

Having to accept such help, while recuperating from my brain injury, also meant I'd been very self-centered. My egocentric attitude had lessened when my daughter was born, but I was still very conscious of what I could and couldn't do.

I was able to breastfeed my daughter on demand, and she moved easily from milk to solids. My fine motor skills were impaired and my hands often shook at inopportune times. I used disposable diapers to avoid having to manipulate safety pins.

The brain injury affected my vision, as well as my balance and coordination. The refocusing mechanism of my eyes was damaged, causing double vision, which I wore glasses to correct. When I was tired, I often had to contend with overlapping images. At those times, I closed my left eye and once I understood what I was looking at, I opened it again. No one even noticed!

No, my difficulties weren't immediately obvious to a casual observer. Loud noises distressed me and confusion upset me. I had refused to let my baby daughter cry for any length of time because it disturbed me, not because I was afraid of harming her psyche.

I snapped out of my reverie and set to work, putting the requisite milk and sugar in the coffee and using a tray to move the mugs to the table. Bryan had made toast. We sat together at the kitchen table, but Meggie stopped after eating half a slice, and got off her chair, saying she wanted to watch TV.

Bryan went to the living room with her. We allowed her to watch public broadcasting stations and the CBC, and she liked the shows they offered. Sesame Street was a favourite, as was Sharon, Lois and Bram. Meggie liked to sing along with their songs, even if she didn't know the words, and I often found myself humming "Skinamarink" or another tune, later in the day. My husband returned to the kitchen and sat down.

"This tea tastes awful," I said, pushing my mug to one side. "I must be pregnant again." The only time I had not wanted to drink tea, my traditional restorative, was when I was pregnant with Meggie.

We had agonized for months, before making the decision to try for another child. The deciding factor had been Christmas 1984.

And Babies Make Seven

It was the second Christmas we'd celebrated in our larger house, and the first that Meggie had been old enough to know about Santa. She opened her stocking by herself, sitting on the floor in front of the decorated tree. We were sitting on the couch, drinking our tea and coffee, trying to pretend we were awake, after being dragged downstairs at 6:00 a.m. Our daughter couldn't wait to see what Santa had left.

"It's sad Meggie doesn't have a sibling to share Christmas with," Bryan observed as he watched her reaching into her stocking. "Opening stockings should happen with a brother or sister so parents can stay in bed for another hour or two."

We discussed the issue each evening, from Christmas Day to New Year's Day, while Bryan was home on holidays. I was used to looking after one child, having done it for two and a half years. Also, I now seemed to have free time, another indication that the time had come to have a second child. I went off the pill.

After two months, *I* thought I was pregnant, but a store-bought pregnancy test indicated I wasn't. But if I *was* pregnant, as my taste buds seemed to indicate…as usual, I was having second thoughts.

I munched my toast, and watched Bryan drinking his coffee. We could hear Meggie singing along with the TV in the living room.

"I know we've decided Meggie needs a brother or sister, and I do agree, but having two children *will* be more work." I said as I took another bite of toast. I didn't add, "for me," but I thought it.

"Yes, but two children will be company for each other, in a couple of years. So soon it'll be less work," replied my husband in his straightforward way. "Maybe you could start writing for the paper again."

"That's true," I mused. Two months previously, I'd quit the column that I'd written for five years.

There Are How Many?

In 1979, when I moved to Peterborough and married Bryan, I'd obtained letters of support from various agencies and groups in the city. Armed with this backing I approached the editor of the local newspaper and suggested that the paper should have a column dealing with disabled people, since 1981 would be the International Year of Disabled Persons.

He hired me. After the birth of my daughter, I took her with me to gather information, which I'd written up in a weekly column. However, after five and a half years and with a two-year-old, the column no longer had top priority. If I had another baby, writing it would definitely be too onerous. But, if I had two children who played together while I collected news over the phone, I might be able to start it again. And according to parenting experts, three years between children was good spacing.

As we made our decision to have another child, we also arranged to put Meggie in nursery school, two mornings a week. She liked going and within a month we increased it to five mornings.

As I finished my toast, I said to Bryan: "It's more expensive sending Meggie to school five days a week. Can we afford another child?"

"Of course we can," he replied. "I earn a good salary, and my job as a software design engineer at Canadian General Electric is secure."

"And then, after this baby, that would be it. Two children would be enough. You could have a vasectomy so I could go off the pill."

Bryan looked at me. "Or you could have your tubes tied."

I knew that's what would happen. Bryan hated medical procedures, but I'd already had many operations and being able to quit taking the pill was worth having another one. I put my dishes on the counter and climbed the stairs. It was time to get dressed. Bryan went to the front room to check on our daughter.

And Babies Make Seven

The next week I went to the doctor's. She performed another pregnancy test and the results confirmed my suspicions. I was glad. It was boring at home while my daughter was at nursery school.

"Since I don't have a profession, or even a job outside the home, raising two children will be my career," I thought.

The doctor said she was sending me for an ultrasound in a couple of weeks. I went home and told Bryan.

"Did she say why?" he asked.

"No, she didn't, and I didn't think to ask. Maybe it's because I had one with Meggie." Many months later, I was able to question my doctor.

"Why *did* you send me for the ultrasound in May?" I asked at a November appointment.

"You were twelve weeks into your pregnancy, but measuring for sixteen," she explained.

"Did you suspect a multiple birth?"

"Not at all. I thought you were out with your dates, and were farther along in your pregnancy than we thought."

In May, my friend and I had speculated on the reason for the ultrasound. We hadn't known my doctor thought I'd miscalculated.

"You do look rather big," she said. "Maybe you're carrying twins."

"Don't be silly," I said. "I can't be."

"Why not? Do twins run in your family?"

"My grandfather had identical twin brothers."

"What about Bryan's family?"

"His dad had non-identical twin aunts. But I still think it's highly unlikely that I'd have twins." I knew nothing about genetics and even less about the propensity for conceiving twins.

13

There Are How Many?

That night I relayed the conversation to my husband. "What do you think, Bryan? Could I be carrying twins?"

"No, of course you're not." And that seemed to settle it.

Two weeks later Bryan and I went to the hospital. I left him sitting in the hall and entered the examination room. I got into the hospital gown, climbed onto the hard table and lay on my back. I thought I knew what to expect but hints indicated this test would be different.

The technician did an initial examination and asked, "Are you on fertility drugs?"

"No," I said. She returned to her work and I didn't want to disturb her. But I did wonder why, if she saw two babies, she didn't just ask me if twins ran in my family. Everyone else did!

"Oh well, maybe she was being technical," I thought. Pretty soon my mind was on other things, like what to have for supper. Had I taken meat out of the freezer? And would Bryan drive me all the way home afterwards or would he drop me off at the corner, on his way back to work, and let me walk the remaining block?

The technician paused in her calculations and turned towards me, asking "Are you comfortable?"

"Oh yes, I'm fine thanks," I replied. Truth be told, I didn't like lying on my back. Ever since my brain injury it made me nauseous to lie in that position, especially when my head was lower than my feet. However, since my head was on a small pillow, I was fine.

I noticed the technician making three entries on a report and I thought, "Triplets? No way! That can't be!"

The technician ran out of the room without saying anything but returned in a few minutes. She continued to make notations, moving the

14

wand to different positions on my belly. After a few more minutes, she stopped, opened the door and invited Bryan to come into the room.

"Do you want to sit down?" she asked him. "I have some important news."

"It's okay. I'm leaning against the table."

A simple sentence, but I heard the unstated frustration. He was probably thinking, "No I bloody well don't want to sit! I've been sitting for nearly an hour. How difficult is it to take a picture of one tiny baby? You didn't even have enough film for crying out loud!"

The technician smiled, looking from my face to Bryan's as she announced. "There are four babies."

2: The Guessing Game

My husband and I looked at each other and started laughing. This was the funniest thing we'd ever heard! As the technician pointed out the four fetuses, we fell silent. I had nearly gone into hysterics. But as the technician pointed out the images, I realized it was true. There really *were* four babies in my belly!

"Yes," I thought. "This sounds like something that might happen to me. After having nearly been killed in a car accident, why not?"

The technician performed the scan again, taking more time to point out the blurry images on the screen. I noticed Bryan watching carefully, and he told me later that he'd checked to see where the wand was each time an image appeared on the screen. However, I didn't think they would have tried to fool us.

Although I had raised my head and was propped on my elbows, I was only slightly more comfortable, and had to turn to see the screen. We could see the babies were in separate sacks and there seemed to be two placentas. The images indicated the babies were all properly formed, all alive, and about three inches long. When the doctor who interprets the ultrasounds came in the room, he agreed there were definitely four babies.

"I've never seen that many babies on one ultrasound," he said.

We left the hospital in a daze. Four babies? Four…babies? It made no sense. Who has four babies at once? Why would we? We didn't even know anyone with twins. We were astounded.

"I can't believe it." Bryan said, opening the door for me as we left the building.

"I know. How could...? Why....? I can't believe it either! What will we do? Are you just going to go back to work?" We were walking to the car as robots, operating on auto pilot.

"No, I think we should do...something—go for tea or something." Bryan paused to unlock the car. He got in and reached to open my door.

"Liz is working today," I said as I slid into the car. "Let's tell her."

"That sounds like a good idea."

Bryan drove out of the lot, across the street and into the parking lot of the Health Unit. We walked around to the side entrance to go straight into the VON office where our friend worked as a nurse.

We knocked on the door to her office and entered when we heard her say, "Come in."

"Hi, Liz. I've just had an ultrasound. Guess how many babies we're going to have?"

"Twins?"

"No, Liz," I said. "There are four babies! We're going to have four babies...at once!"

"Are you serious?" She asked, looking from my face to Bryan's. She knew he liked to joke.

"It's true, Liz." said Bryan.

"Wow! Really? That's amazing!" She said, trying not to shriek.

"I know. We can hardly believe it." I said, and started laughing.

The three of us stood there, grinning at each other. Liz was shaking her head. Bryan and I were nodding ours.

"No, it can't be," she seemed to say.

"Yes, it is," we appeared to be nodding in reply.

She gave me a hug. "Wow, Val, this is so unexpected!"

That was one way of putting it. We talked for a bit longer, but we didn't want to keep our friend from her work. As we left, I turned to wave. She was still standing in the middle of her office shaking her head but she waved back.

Bryan drove me home. "I'm going to go back to work now."

"Okay. You can play the 'guess how many babies we're going to have' game."

"Yeah, I don't know how much work I'll get done."

As soon as Bryan left, I walked down the street to get Meggie at my friend's. I saw Mary sitting on her front lawn, enjoying the sunshine. I held up four fingers. She smiled and called, "I thought so. You're four months, aren't you?"

"No, Mary, there are four babies."

"Oh my God!"

I motioned to Meggie who, with Mary's daughter, was rolling down the grassy incline to the sidewalk.

"Come, Meggie. It's time to go home." She ran over to me, and I took her hand. Standing in front of Mary, I thanked her for looking after my daughter.

"I was happy to do it," she said, smiling. "Four babies. Wow!"

I waved and started to walk home, with Meggie beside me, still thinking about the news. I could've been told I had fifteen babies in my belly. It would've made as much sense. It was ironic—I had wondered if I'd be able to cope with two children and now it seemed I would have five.

After Meggie and I arrived at the house, I put on a Sharon, Lois and Bram tape. My daughter climbed onto a chair at the dining room table, knelt and opened a colouring book. Bouncing side to side, in beat with the music, she selected a red crayon.

Satisfied that my daughter was occupied for a while, I went into the family room to phone my doctor.

"I've just come from the ultrasound, and guess what?"

The nurse was quiet for a moment, and then asked, "What?"

"I'm going to have four babies."

After expressing surprise and concern, she said she'd tell the doctor and asked if I wanted to go to the same obstetrician I'd gone to for my first pregnancy.

"Oh yes. Bryan and I both liked him."

She said she'd ask his office to phone with an appointment time and offered her congratulations. I thanked her and we hung up.

That night, after we'd eaten dinner and put Meggie to bed, we made a series of long-distance phone calls. We called Bryan's father and stepmother, his two sisters and his brother, both my brothers and two of my aunts. The response to our announcement was a variation of the one we'd gotten all day: "Oh my goodness!" and "How amazing!"

My parents were holidaying overseas and weren't expected home for two weeks. We wanted to wait to contact them since we knew my mother would be eager to get home after she heard the news. I wrote to the friend they'd be visiting in England before their flight home.

When my mother received the letter the next week, she phoned immediately. She couldn't wait to get back and I had to reassure her several times that I was okay, Meggie was fine, and the doctors had everything under control.

Meanwhile, the morning after telling our families, I told Meggie. At age three, she wasn't very excited. Her world didn't include thoughts of siblings, no matter how many there were. Later that day, I mentioned Meggie's reaction, or lack thereof, to Bryan.

"I'll go to the library to get a children's book with quadruplets in the story, if there is one. Maybe reading it to her will help."

"It's worth a try. See what you can find," he replied.

A couple of weeks later, we were sitting outside, enjoying the late afternoon sunshine. It was early June but still cool enough to need sweaters. Bryan had just assembled the swing set we'd bought Meggie for her third birthday. It had three swings, a glider and a slide—enough for five children. He started to gather the tools.

"Come, Meggie. You can play on the swings tomorrow. Let's go inside now."

A couple of days later, I searched the children's section of the library, and found one book with quadruplets in the story. A little girl had identical quadruplet baby brothers, and she was upset because she couldn't tell them apart. After looking at each baby carefully, however, she was able to discover a distinguishing feature for each baby. The book ended with her being happy that her brothers, although looking the same, were not *exactly* the same.

I wondered if it would happen like that for my daughter. What if *we* had four identical babies? How would we tell them apart?

After I finished reading, I said to Meggie, "This is how many brothers or sisters you're going to have." She looked at me and smiled, but the story had ended. She got off my lap.

That night as we were getting ready for bed, I said to Bryan, "I don't think reading the story to Meggie helped. She still doesn't seem to understand what's happening."

"That's not surprising. She's only three years old, for heaven's sake. We barely understand it. Why should she?"

Over the next couple of days, however, as we discussed the astounding news, I realized that Bryan and I also differed in our reactions.

My first thought was to my physical ability—how would I get through the pregnancy? Next, I worried about the effect having four siblings at once would have on Meggie. Bryan, I discovered, was more concerned with practical matters.

"I can't even fit both of us and four babies in the car," he said one day as we were watching TV. We drove a 1980 BMW. "You know what this means—one of my worst fears of being married has come true. I'll have to buy a van!"

Cars were Bryan's hobby. He loved sporty cars, classic cars, and expensive cars. Vans, on the other hand, were not what car enthusiasts drove. It was impossible to sit around fantasizing about...vans. Nobody drooled over...vans. No, driving a van was going to be a disappointment.

"Boo-hoo." Bryan feigned crying after finishing his van diatribe.

I encircled him with my arms, and in a fake gesture of sympathy patted his back. Then we both laughed. Bryan's next comment, a suggestion to go out that weekend and buy a microwave oven, indicated again his concern with practical matters.

"Why would we do that?" I knew he had been looking for an excuse to buy one. As soon as a new technology was available, Bryan wanted to own it.

"If you're tired all the time, and I have to come home from work and cook dinner, I'll be able to defrost meat and cook it quickly."

"That makes sense," I said. "Maybe we should buy one."

The Guessing Game

The show we'd been watching ended and Bryan turned off the TV. As we headed up the stairs, he asked about visiting the doctor.

"I'm going to see an obstetrician next week. You'll be able to come with me, won't you?"

"Yes, I can take time off work."

We got ready for bed and my last thought as I fell asleep was of my daughter, wondering whether she'd like to have brothers, sisters, or a mixture of each.

A few days later, we were at a restaurant, standing in line for the buffet. Being noticeably pregnant by this time, strangers often mistook my girth for impending birth. A woman behind me in the line asked when I was due. I explained that I was only four months, and it was the number of babies I was carrying that accounted for my size.

"Imagine that!" she said to her husband.

"No," he said. "I don't think I want to!"

We all laughed. As Bryan talked further with them, we discovered they had a van for sale. It was a well-used, nine-year-old Dodge Sportsman maxi van that seated nine, with a 400 cubic inch engine. It only got 10 miles to the gallon, quite a bit worse than the BMW, but Bryan thought it would suit us. We arranged to buy it. It was our first step into our new life.

Our new life in which, if all went well, we'd have a few more children than planned. We'd laughed when we'd first received the news but reality was starting to sink in. Would we still be laughing after our first visit to the obstetrician?

3: Hurry Up and Wait

I sat in the obstetrician's office, trying to absorb the news.

"Val will have to give birth in Toronto," the doctor had said. "I wouldn't even try to handle it here."

I was so distressed at this I barely heard the reason: the local hospital was a secondary care centre and I'd need a tertiary one.

"I don't want to go to Toronto!" I thought. I'd lived in this city for six years. It was my home. Toronto was only a two-hour drive away but it wasn't a journey we undertook often.

"The hospital here could monitor you closely," he said, "with visits to Toronto every couple of weeks for the doctors at Women's College Hospital to watch the growth of the babies. Then as the due date drew near, you'd have to go into that hospital.

"Constant observation is necessary," he continued, "because one of the risks of multiple birth pregnancies is that one of the babies could fall behind the others. If it appears that one is failing so much that he may die, then the decision must be made: do you save the one and put the other three at risk because they'll be born prematurely, or do you sacrifice the one for the benefit of the remaining three?

"If tests indicate one of the babies is lagging behind, then you might have to go on complete bed rest to allow all your nutrients to be made available to them. I'll phone the hospital tomorrow."

"Sounds good," said Bryan. I stayed silent, still trying to grasp what the doctor had said.

"I don't want to go to a hospital in Toronto." The thought ran through my head like a refrain.

The doctor resumed talking. "As well, the babies will likely be quite premature and you'll have to have a C-section. Make an appointment to come back tomorrow. I'll know more then."

"Okay. Thanks." Bryan shook the doctor's hand and I did too. We spoke to the nurse before leaving, making our next appointment.

"I have to admit that I was a little nervous about the visit, wondering what he would say," said Bryan as we left. "But it might not be that bad."

"Maybe..." I paused, concentrating on going down the stairs. I held Bryan's arm on one side and the railing on the other. I needed the extra support; my mind occupied with thoughts of leaving town. Having the caesarean didn't upset me nearly as much because I'd already experienced a completely natural birth with my daughter.

"We'll have to see what the other doctors say, of course," said Bryan as he held the door open. "But I could get time off work to drive you to Toronto every couple of weeks."

"I want to give birth here, in this city. I like this hospital. It's where Meggie was born." I protested, as we left the building and walked to the car.

"I know, Val, but if they don't have the machines here that the babies will need to keep them alive, we'll have to go to a place that does." Bryan got in on one side as I went to the other.

"Yes, I guess you're right." I still wasn't happy at the thought of going into the big city, though. I buckled my seat belt.

And Babies Make Seven

"Who would look after Meggie?" I wondered as we drove home.

The next day, when we returned to the physician's office, we were stunned to discover what the doctors had recommended.

I was to be put on full bed rest in seven weeks. A month later, at week 25 of my pregnancy, the earliest time the babies could be born with any hope of survival, I was to be sent to the hospital in Toronto to wait until the babies were delivered by caesarean birth.

Suddenly this wasn't a game anymore. The ground had shifted, the rules had changed, and we were in a new reality. How could I care for our daughter? Bryan and I would be separated for weeks. Our frustration was palpable.

My husband, I knew, was trained to solve problems as they arose, to find solutions, to act. What sort of solution could he find in this instance? What action could he take? There wasn't anything he could do.

What could I do? I would be back in the hospital, but instead of waiting for my body to heal, I'd be waiting while four new lives grew within me.

"Here we go again," I thought. But this wasn't a tragedy, it was a joyous event. I didn't feel very joyful yet, though.

We left the doctor's office without talking. What was there to say? We both knew what we had to do, even if we didn't like it. Meanwhile, Bryan had his job to do and I had to revise my life plan. It wouldn't be two children playing together while I was on the phone collecting information for my column, that's for sure!

A couple of days later, I answered a knock at the door. It was a public health nurse. My doctor, after hearing my news, had arranged for her to visit.

"How do you feel?" she asked after we'd introduced ourselves and taken a seat in the living room.

I didn't know what to say. How *did* I feel? I remembered telling Meggie's teacher at nursery school a day earlier, and her reaction.

"Oh Val, how exciting—natural quadruplets!" she'd exclaimed, taking both my hands in hers.

I borrowed her response in replying to the nurse. "I'm excited, I guess." I paused, and then added, "But it's kind of scary too."

"The books I've read suggest you wait to set up a nursery until after the babies are born. They'll likely be quite premature and you'll have time before they all come home. Also, you'll want to wait to make sure they're healthy."

"Oh," I hadn't thought about that. "That makes sense, I guess."

We talked a bit more about nutrition, and general pregnancy topics. Only three years had passed since I'd been pregnant with Meggie, and I recalled the admonitions: no smoking (I didn't anyway), and limiting my alcoholic intake (also not a problem).

After she left, I phoned information at the library to ask about a local multiple births' organization. I discovered there was a twins club.

"The group's name is SPOT-Support for Parents of Twins. They meet the third Thursday of each month, at a member's home. There's a contact and phone number. Do you want them?" asked the librarian.

"Yes, please."

I wrote both down and after hanging up, checked the phone book. The address was a couple of blocks away. I dialled the number and a woman answered. After introducing myself, I told her my news. She was a mother of twins and calmly offered her congratulations.

"Our group is meeting next Thursday at my house," she added. "Will you be able to come?"

"Yes, I'd like to," I replied. "Can my husband come too?"

"Yes. He might be the only one here, though, because husbands don't usually come." she said. "But he's more than welcome to be here."

"Okay. I'll tell Bryan. Thanks."

We said good-bye and hung up. That evening at dinner, I told Bryan about the nurse's visit and the news about the twins club.

"I guess we have to be prepared for the babies not being healthy when they're born."

"There's a chance, I guess. But we'll deal with that if and when it happens. Right now we won't anticipate problems."

Yes, that was the way I wanted to think about it too. Everything going well was enough to consider. If I had to start anticipating what we'd do if things went bad...I couldn't do it. The power of positive thinking would be my motto. I'd already dealt with tragedy and I could do it again if need be. Dealing with a momentous, *joyous* occasion was "something completely different" to quote Monty Python.

"The public health nurse said we'll have time to set up a nursery after the babies are born. That's one thing we don't have to worry about right now.

"The twins club meets next Thursday. I'd like to go, just to meet people and talk to others who have twins. There isn't anybody in town with quadruplets."

"Yet..." said Bryan, and he laughed.

"Yes," I said, smiling. "Will you come to the meeting with me? Husbands don't usually attend and you might be the only one there."

Hurry Up and Wait

"I guess I could come..." he said. He tried to convey ambivalence, but I knew he'd be pleased to go. He'd want to talk to others about our news. One of the reasons our marriage worked well was that Bryan liked to talk and I was happy to let him.

Several weeks later, I was admitted to the local hospital. My doctor wanted to put me on a drug that reduced the chance of going into premature labour. Since a side effect was the possibility of affecting a person's blood pressure, I had to be monitored closely.

We left our daughter at home with a babysitter while my husband drove me to the hospital. After I was admitted, we kissed each other goodbye, and he left.

Both my husband and I were familiar with hospitals, having had to go into them as either a patient or a visitor as teenagers. In 1971, Bryan's mother had been in a hospital for several weeks before succumbing to cancer. My hospital stay had resulted in a new life for me, but Bryan's experience had dealt with death.

During his visits to me, the hospital smells could trigger painful memories. Still, Bryan knew why I had to be in the hospital, even if it made him uncomfortable. I was more concerned about my daughter, who wouldn't understand why I couldn't be at home with her.

Bryan came to have lunch with me the next day. He'd brought a sandwich, and after he'd eaten, I suggested we go outside. I wanted to hear how Meggie was doing.

It was a mild day, with a bright sun. I resented being in the hospital in the summer, but it was refreshing to walk outside and smell the trees and grass. I linked arms with Bryan, not because I needed support, but as a gesture of love.

"It's only been one day, but how is Meggie? Does she miss me?"

"I'm sure she does," Bryan said, smiling. "I got up at seven and got dressed. Then I went into her bedroom to get her clothes. When I tried to choose an outfit, she began crying, saying 'Mummy lets me do it!'"

"Oh dear. Poor Meggie." Seeing him open his mouth to protest, I added, "And poor Bryan, too. You're not at your best in the morning, are you? It won't be much longer, though. I'll be home by Friday."

"It'll be good to have you home again. Fortunately, Meggie doesn't seem to mind going to the babysitter's."

We'd made that decision before I'd gone into the hospital. We knew a woman who had worked in a store I shopped at regularly and who now took children into her home. Since she lived close to both the hospital and Bryan's workplace, it seemed an ideal solution.

Bryan left shortly after we returned to my room, promising to visit again later with Meggie. After my excursion outside, I got back into bed and resumed my patient status.

I had another ultrasound that afternoon. In one month, the babies had grown to almost twice their original size. The four weights were within a hundred grams, indicating their growth rates were similar.

Shortly after 5:00 p.m., I heard my daughter.

"Mummy! Mummy!" She tried to hurry Bryan into my room as soon as she saw me. I sat up and swung my feet off the bed. My tummy was bigger than normal, but I could still move quite easily.

Meggie climbed onto the bed, and I hugged her. It felt good to put my arms around her and hold her close. She smelled sweet—like vanilla ice cream. Bryan and I joined hands briefly while my daughter made herself comfortable on my lap. While she sat there, I smoothed her hair.

"What did you do at the babysitter's today?"

"I played with two dollies, and we had a tea party in the back yard. It was a pretend party, but we had ice cream."

"I thought so!"

I showed Bryan the piece of paper with the results of the ultrasound. He looked at it and after a minute put it in his pocket. I knew he would add the data to the chart he was keeping on the computer at home. Keeping track of such things was something concrete that he could do. I assumed it made him feel better, giving him a sense of control.

Meggie climbed off my lap and walked to the window, but it was too high for her to look out. She was restless and walked from the bed to the window and back several times.

"We'd better go," Bryan said. "Say good-bye to Mummy. We'll come back tomorrow for another visit."

"Bye-bye sweetie. I'll be home in a few days." I reached down and pulled her close to give her a kiss.

"Bye Mummy." She gave me a kiss on the cheek.

I stood and watched as they left the room. Bryan was holding Meggie's hand, and she was skipping at his side. I was glad she'd started going to nursery school in January. It had prepared her, if only slightly, for our separation.

When I came home from the hospital in the first week of July, I weighed 166 pounds and my waist was forty-three inches. I'd put on thirty-five pounds and my waistline had increased by seventeen inches. I was only five months pregnant, just over halfway through a term pregnancy. For my first pregnancy, I'd gained fifty pounds.

It was the weekend, and Bryan was home. I helped as much as I could, without standing, since that was forbidden. Stairs were also out-of-bounds. I was only allowed go up and down them once a day. Since the only bathroom was upstairs, we had to get a commode chair. We obtained one from the Red Cross.

I had used a commode chair in 1970, and didn't think doing so again was unusual. Bryan, on the other hand, found it disconcerting, especially when he was the one who had to empty it.

On Sunday night, my parents arrived and my mother was able to take over many of the household tasks. We made up the bed chesterfield in the family room and I spent most of the day lying there. I was able to tell Mom where things were and we planned meals together. My dad stayed for a few days, but then he had to return to his parish.

Meggie was on summer vacation from nursery school. But instead of enjoying this time with my daughter, I gave the impression of being sick. I was horizontal for most of the day, and I visited the doctor weekly.

At one visit Bryan asked, "What will happen if Val goes into labour in the next week or two?"

"If you do," the doctor replied, looking at me, "the doctors will make no heroic efforts to save the babies. They'd be too young to survive without respirators and we don't have any in Peterborough. But the hospital in Toronto has equipment to keep very premature babies alive."

"That's good to know. I don't want to go into Toronto, but I guess I'm going to have to do what's best for the babies." I looked at Bryan and shrugged. He smiled; he understood.

After thanking the doctor, we left and drove home. Mom had dinner ready, and we appreciated not having to rush home and prepare a meal. That night, after we'd put Meggie to bed, we told Mom what the doctor had said.

"We don't want to have to send Meggie to the babysitter's for that length of time," I said. "Could she live with you while I'm in Toronto?"

"Yes, of course. We'd be happy to have her."

Bryan and I thanked her.

The next day, during our noon time phone call, Bryan told me about a call he'd made that morning.

"I talked to a woman in the States, the president of a group organized for people who have triplets and quadruplets or supertwins as they're called. She said that women who gain seventy to ninety pounds during their pregnancy and who have lots of bed rest are more successful with their quads.

"Also, she agrees with the doctor's decision to use the level III center in Toronto, because having the increased care results in a better success rate for the babies. Bed rest for the mother is important as well, to guard against the weight of the babies triggering labour."

So I was doing the right thing, it seemed--lying around the house, with occasional forays into the side yard to sit in the sun. It reminded me of the time I'd spent convalescing before, when I'd been physically unable to walk. Now I wasn't supposed to, but the effect was the same.

At my next doctor's appointment, he did an internal examination and discovered that my cervix was starting to dilate, although it was still hard. The doctor had to leave before he could explain what that meant, and we were worried, although obviously he wasn't.

After talking with friends who were nurses, however, we felt better. The condition of my cervix indicated that bed rest was required, and resting in bed is what I was doing.

The next day, a reporter from our local paper phoned.

"Hello. I hear you're expecting quadruplets. Can I come over to interview you?"

I was hesitant to say yes without asking Bryan first. I asked her to phone him.

"Sure." She said. "What's his number?"

I told her and we hung up. Within minutes the phone rang again.

"We don't want this reported in the paper." Bryan sounded angry.

"I used to write for the Examiner and I want them to get the story," I replied.

"I think it's too early to start talking about it," he responded. "But she'll want to talk to the doctor. I'll phone him to see what he thinks. I'll call you back."

We hung up. I was surprised at Bryan's reaction. Even writing an events column as I had done, I knew the value of being the first to report a newsworthy item. Five minutes later the phone rang again.

"I talked to the doctor." Bryan seemed more composed this time. "He is unwilling to talk to the media until after the babies are born, because if the story comes out now and something goes wrong at the birth, we'll be expected to answer questions at a bad time. He suggested we let her write the story now but not print it until after the babies are born. Can you phone and tell her?"

"Sure. That'll keep everyone happy."

After we hung up I phoned the paper and arranged for the reporter to come over Saturday afternoon.

A week later, on July 20, I hugged my mother and kissed my sweet daughter good-bye, before Bryan drove them to the station to catch the train to London, where my father would meet them. I knew from the look on Bryan's face that he was going to find it difficult saying good-bye to his little Meggie.

Hurry Up and Wait

The next day, I was admitted to the local hospital to wait until Tuesday, the day I was to be transported to Toronto.

Two months had passed since discovering we were going to have quadruplets. Our initial reaction had been laughter, but it was really a form of shock. Then after the trip to the obstetrician, we'd been stunned and dismayed to discover what was to come. But through all that, we'd been together. Our team approach had been our comfort.

The next phase of our happy event would separate us. I would be in the hospital in the city, dealing with the physical aspects of the impending birth. Bryan, who had always been my anchor and my mainstay, would be at home alone. And our daughter, who had never been away from us for more than a weekend, would be living with her grandparents in an entirely different city. How would we all manage?

4: Let It Be Over

Tuesday morning I awoke early, eager to get on with our adventure. Giving birth at the hospital in the city, which had been an obstacle at first, now seemed like the natural next step. We had accepted our situation, and were anticipating a successful birth.

"Oh, good, you're early," I said as Bryan entered my room just before 8:00 a.m.

"How was your breakfast?" He asked, noticing the empty tray.

"Good. Come and sit."

I patted the bed and he sat so we could hug and kiss. His familiar scent cheered me. I didn't want to be away from him, and I sensed he felt the same. But, que sera, sera—we couldn't back out now.

Bryan retrieved the suitcase from the locker beside my bed and took my clothes from the hangers. After packing my bag, Bryan accompanied me to the nurses' station so I could say goodbye and thank-you to the nurses who had cared for me.

"Good-bye, Mrs. Keelan. I wish you could have the babies here."

"Yes," I said. "I'd prefer that too but I have to do what's best for the babies." (That was my rallying cry.)

The nurses smiled, and even the housekeeping staff looked pleased. Everyone was so cheerful that our spirits began to lift. This *was* exciting. We went back to my room. A few minutes later, two ambulance attendants rolled a gurney into my room and helped me onto it.

Bryan carried my suitcase, and we all got on the elevator. At the emergency entrance, they wheeled me outside and loaded me into the waiting ambulance. Bryan got in through the passenger door and sat on the jump seat by my head.

"We have to stop to pick up another patient," the driver explained.

After a ten-minute ride through town, we parked at the other hospital, and the attendants went in. They returned in a few minutes and told us there was a problem.

"We'll take her out and you can sit with her in emerg while we get this straightened out," one of them said to Bryan as he pulled the stretcher out of the vehicle. The orderlies wheeled me into the building, and Bryan pulled a chair over so we could talk.

"I'm glad to be out of there," I said. "I was feeling quite sick."

"I'll tell them," he said. "Maybe if they put you in the other way around it'll help."

Listening to the talk around us, we discovered that the other patient was unstable, violent, and wearing bandages around his hands to prevent him from hitting himself and others. He was drugged, but once the drugs wore off, his actions would be unpredictable.

"What do you think will happen now?" I asked Bryan.

"I don't know."

After another ten minutes of waiting, he nodded at a man standing on the other side of the room.

"I'll go ask him. He drove us here."

I watched as Bryan crossed the room and spoke to a man in uniform. After a few minutes, he returned.

"He doesn't know what's happening either but he said there was no way he was going to drive you to Toronto with a guy who might be uncontrollable. He also said another ambulance crew should be coming to take us back to the other hospital."

A while later, the ambulance driver approached. "We'll take you back since it doesn't appear another crew is coming."

"Okay," said Bryan, "but Val gets car sick. Can you put her in the other way around to see if it helps?"

"Sure."

After they'd put me in the ambulance, and with Bryan seated at my feet, I whispered, "Thanks, Bry!"

He smiled. It was a disappointment, returning to the first medical facility after we'd said goodbye but I did discover that when I was facing frontward I didn't feel queasy. It wasn't a wasted trip after all.

After spending twenty minutes in the emergency room, Bryan became impatient.

"I'm going back to work. Phone me when they make a decision."

"I will. It's probably better if you get some work done."

We smiled at each other and Bryan left. I was taken upstairs to the room I'd left that morning. Left alone, I slipped into hospital mode-- lying in bed, listening to the machines, the public address system, and the nurses talking.

At lunch, I was given a tray of food, which I ate. My appetite was increasing along with my waistline.

At 3:00 p.m., I phoned my husband. "Bry, can you come back to the hospital? I'm just lying here. Nothing has been decided."

"OK. It's almost quitting time. I'll be up in twenty minutes."

When Bryan arrived, we were given the following possibilities: an ambulance crew could take us at 4:30 p.m.; the air ambulance might be available at 6:00 p.m., or we could go at 10:00 a.m. the next day.

Let it Be Over

If we decided to use the air ambulance, it would only take twenty minutes, but it was unreliable since we weren't an emergency. In addition, Bryan would not be able to go. Since we'd been counting on going together, that was a mark against that option. We did not want to wait another day; we decided to take the 4:30 p.m. option.

I dozed for most of the trip, but between naps, I thought about life in a hospital. The world shrinks; meals and treatment times become the centre of the universe. I'd lived in a microcosm before and hadn't minded. In some ways, I was an ideal patient.

When we arrived at the hospital after an uneventful ride, I was taken to a room for an initial examination. Afterwards, Bryan joined me.

"That was quick," Bryan said, reaching out to hold my hand. I was still lying on a gurney.

"I know. She just checked my blood pressure and pulse. She didn't try to monitor the babies."

A nurse appeared with a clipboard in hand. "Hi. My name is Mary. I'll be taking care of you, and will be back in two minutes."

Two minutes came and went. Ten minutes came and went. I dozed while Bryan read the book he had with him for the ride home. He checked his watch.

"I'm going to have to catch the bus, Val. I don't want to just leave you here though."

"That's OK. You don't want to be late. They won't forget I'm here." I said and smiled, trying to look brave.

"Okay. I'll remind someone about you, on my way out. I'll phone tomorrow to see how things are going."

And Babies Make Seven

Bryan bent down to kiss me and I reached up to hug him. We held each other briefly, and then he pulled away. He turned and waved before walking through the doorway.

Shortly after he left, another nurse came in and took me to a room with three occupied beds and one empty one. I eased myself off the stretcher and onto it, with help from the nurse. I prepared for bed without waking the mothers in the other beds, and went to sleep.

The next afternoon I was given a private room. It was a pleasant, spacious room with a private two-piece bathroom, but the window looked out on a roof and a brick wall. There was no mistaking it as a hospital room, however, with its antiseptic smell. The charge nurse told me that because I had a private room, due to the number of babies I was expecting Bryan could come for weekend visits. A cot was placed in my room.

I put my suitcase in the locker, and sat on the bed. A nurse arrived with a wheelchair and took me to another room. I sat on the examining table, and she helped me lift my feet.

"I have to smear this Vaseline-type stuff over your belly. Have you had a non-stress test before?" The technician asked.

"I don't know. I've had ultrasounds. What's the difference?"

"This test measures the fetal heart rate in relation to the contractions; the ultrasound is a picture of the fetuses. I'll fasten these two belts around you." The technician explained her actions as she worked.

"The belts will measure the heart rate of the fetus in response to its own movements for twenty to thirty minutes. Measuring fetal activity in this way helps to determine if oxygen levels are adequate. It tells the doctors how the fetuses are doing."

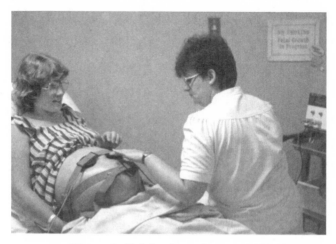

Figure 1: Val having a "non-stress" test

After the procedure was finished, I was wheeled back to my room. Instead of resting, I walked to a common area at the end of the hall. Other mothers, in all stages of pregnancy, were reading or talking in groups.

We were all high-risk births, but the reasons for that status varied. Between excursions to examining rooms, we traded stories. Some women had medical conditions affecting their pregnancies, and one woman was expecting triplets. It was her fist pregnancy and she was in her thirties. I was the only one expecting quadruplets, though.

I was overjoyed to see Bryan when he came to visit three days later. The next morning I suggested we go for a walk.

"You'll have to ask the nurses if I can go out," I added.

Bryan left, but I could hear him talking in the hall. A few minutes later, he came back.

"We can go downstairs to the foyer and we can go outside to the front lawn to sit in the sunshine. But that's as far as we can go."

"It'll be a change from being in here."

And Babies Make Seven

Sitting on a bench, smelling the fresh scent of newly mown grass, mixed with the not-so-fresh scent of car exhaust, Bryan and I discussed the results of the ultrasound I'd had earlier in the week.

"The babies are between 690 and 820 grams," he said. "The nurse I spoke to said that's a very good sign. We don't have to worry yet about one lagging behind."

"That's good to know." I said.

We sat holding hands for a few more minutes. Bryan told me how much he missed both Meggie and me. He had spent a couple of evenings sitting in the dark, listening to Joni Mitchell albums, reliving the grief he'd felt when his mother had died. I reassured him that I wasn't going to die, but I, too, was still trying to absorb the joy of this event. We were silent for a few minutes, each pondering our own perspective.

"I'm ready to go back to my room," I said.

Bryan and I began the slow trek back. The weekend visit was over all too quickly and we had to live apart for another week.

On Friday, when Bryan arrived for his next visit, he said, "Tomorrow's the Caribbana Parade, and it starts a block from here. I'll ask if we can walk over to watch it."

"Okay. That'll be fun."

The doctor agreed I could go but I had to be in a wheelchair. The next day, I thought, "I hope this isn't going to happen every fifteen years."

Bryan stood beside me on the sidewalk, watching the floats with dancers in their brightly coloured garb, and listening to the reggae and calypso bands. The summer breeze was a welcome relief to the medicinal odour that my nose normally smelled.

The parade moved past us and disappeared down the street. Bryan pushed me back to the hospital and took me to my room. That was my last big excursion. In the remaining weeks before my babies' birth, I would be unable to leave the building.

The doctors wanted my pregnancy to last thirty-two weeks but secretly Bryan and I wished for something shorter. We hoped I wouldn't go into labour until at least week twenty-eight, so the babies would have a good chance of surviving, but we were also impatient and wanted the birth to happen as soon as possible.

I had been in the hospital nearly three weeks when we were given a tour of delivery room eleven, the one appointed for my C-section. It was very large, since it had to accommodate many people: a surgeon and an assistant for each baby, a scrub nurse, a circulating nurse, and an anesthesiologist. I added them in my head: eight, nine, ten, eleven. If my doctors from Peterborough came, there could be fifteen people present.

"The birth will take about fifteen minutes, and closing the incision will take another hour," said our tour guide. We followed her into another room filled with incubators.

"This is the Neonatal Intensive Care Unit, the NICU." She moved to an incubator and pointed. "This baby weighed 630 grams when it was born yesterday, at twenty-six weeks."

Bryan and I looked at the scrawny, wrinkled form that was still recognizable as a baby, and then at each other.

"Our babies weigh more than that now," he said. "So there's a good chance ours will survive, even if they're born soon."

We continued moving, following the nurse. We looked at each incubator as we passed. I could hardly believe that I had four such beings inside me already, although looking down at my huge stomach, maybe it wasn't that incredible. I pulled my thoughts back to the nurse, talking about the upcoming birth.

"Your husband can stay with you while they're finishing the operation and then you'll be wheeled through the nursery so you can see the newborns too. You'll be in intermediate intensive care for a few hours and then you'll be taken back to your room." We stopped before we left the NICU to remove our gowns.

"How long will it be before the babies are able to come home?" I asked as we started down the hall, Bryan pushing me in a wheelchair.

"The babes will stay in a hospital, either here or in Peterborough, until their due date or until they are five pounds (2300 grams) and big enough to go home."

"Their due date is November 7. If they're born in the next few weeks, it'll be several months before they come home." I said.

"Yes," said Bryan. "And maybe by then we'll be ready for them!"

I laughed. "Or we may never be. We may just have to wing it."

"That sounds more likely," Bryan agreed, laughing.

We entered my room, but the nurse continued walking down the hall. I rested on the bed, but Bryan left after a few minutes to go to the cafeteria. When he returned, a half hour later, my food had arrived. He sat and read while I finished eating.

The next day was Sunday. Bryan wheeled me to the foyer and back, but that was as far as I could go. In the remaining weeks, my activity would be further limited until I wouldn't be able to leave the ward.

Three more weeks passed. Bryan and I were together for the weekends, but we lived separate weekday lives. He phoned the hospital daily to receive updates on the growth of the babies. During our regular Wednesday phone calls, he and I discussed what he had learned.

"The three little ones are gaining about twenty grams a day, and the bigger one is gaining twenty-six grams a day," he said. "They seem to

be on the growth curve for normal singletons, which I find surprising. I
would've thought that because they're smaller, and there's more than one,
they wouldn't grow as quickly."

"That would make sense to me," I agreed. "But I guess that's not
how it works."

During one of Bryan's visits, I waddled to the weigh scale at the
end of the hall. I weighed 80.6 kg, or 179 lbs. We used a tape measure
around my waist: 47.5 inches. In a month I'd put on thirteen pounds, and
added four inches to my waist.

"It's no wonder," I explained. "I eat six times a day. When I wake
up in the middle of the night, I ask the nurse for my bedtime snack. She
gets the paper bag that is stored in the fridge."

"Oh great," Bryan said. "I hope that's not going to continue after
the babies are born."

"I hope not either."

During one of our midweek conversations, I asked Bryan if he had
been able to organize any help.

"No, I've talked to a few people at city hall. The only suggestion
so far is to contact social service agencies."

"What'll we do if we can't get any help? How will we manage?"

"Instead of supervising other people, we'll have to do the work."

"I can't look after four babies at once," I snapped. Who did he
think I was, Superwoman?

Bryan, ever the patient teacher, tried to calm me: "You won't have
to. You'll just have to take care of one at a time. There will be economies
of scale. Caring for four won't be four times the work of caring for one.

"I've discovered that neither the federal nor the provincial
governments are able to offer any help. It appears you have to have five

babies at once for that. We just didn't have enough babies to qualify." He paused. "Maybe we should try again!"

"No way!" I screeched, before I realized he was teasing.

Bryan became serious again, reminding me that our capabilities had previously expanded to meet our needs.

"Remember how, before Meggie was born, we hadn't known whether you could handle one child? But until recently you've been taking care of her, writing a weekly newspaper column, and managing the household as well."

"I guess you're right," I replied reluctantly. I was in no mood to think positively; I was getting grouchier as I grew larger.

A week later, the ultrasound showed that the babes were all over two pounds. They had gained thirty-one to thirty-three grams a day for the previous two weeks. The non-stress tests, taken twice weekly, were showing good results indicating that the babies were developing normally.

I was becoming very uncomfortable, but when I asked if I could be scheduled for a C-section, a nurse told me: "The longer you wait, the better it'll be for the babes. I know it's hard on you now, but it really is much better to wait as long as possible. The bigger the babies are when they're born, the better their chances of survival."

At an examination the next day, my cervix was four centimetres dilated and seventy-percent effaced, indicating my body was readying itself to start labour. The next day I was checked again since I was still having tightenings, or pre-contractions, but there was no change.

When Bryan arrived later that day for his weekend visit, we decided to track the pains since they seemed to be getting regular. We stayed awake until 4:00 a.m. Saturday morning, calling the nurse each time I felt a spasm.

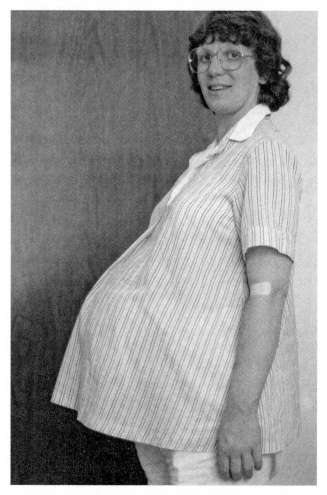

Figure 2: Val and the boys

This caused great excitement. The nursery was prepared, and the medical personnel were paying attention. When a monitor was attached, however, the pains died down and stopped. We were very disappointed.

The next morning, the doctors did another examination and found that my cervix hadn't changed. If it had dilated one more centimeter, I was told later, the doctors would have done the operation that afternoon. However, as long as my body was waiting, it seemed prudent for us to wait as well.

An examination on Monday found that the weekend activity had changed my cervix and even though it was still thick, it had dilated to five centimetres. The doctor left, and a few minutes later a nurse came in to tell me the operation was scheduled for the next day at 10:00 a.m.

Bryan had gone back to Peterborough the night before, and I phoned him with the exciting news. He came back to Toronto that evening, and planned to spend a few days. We were almost too excited to sleep, so relieved were we that the waiting was finally over.

5: Two Minutes to Seven

I opened my eyes and looked at my husband in the cot across the room. After three long months, my sons' birthday, August 27, had finally arrived. I knew we had several hours to wait, but I wanted to be up and at 'em—figuratively speaking, of course. I was so big and cumbersome I wasn't about to go anywhere or do anything. Bryan opened his eyes.

"Well, we made it. This is the day." I said, expecting some humourous rejoinder, as was his usual, but he just smiled.

"Yup, we made it. I'll get up now." He got off his cot and went into the bathroom. A few minutes later, he went down to the cafeteria. He knew the nurses would be in soon and it was best to be gone.

After he left, I thought about our relationship. Since meeting Bryan seven years ago, I had had an uncanny sense that we belonged together, that our marriage was inevitable. We rarely disagreed, but when we did, we talked our problems out, and usually ended up laughing.

One of Bryan's friends at work had joked that if he'd discovered his wife was expecting quadruplets, he would've bought a one-way ticket to Buenos Aires. We chuckled at that because it was preposterous to think that Bryan would leave me alone with five children. We would face whatever the future held, together.

I turned my thoughts to the breakfast tray that had just arrived. Since I was having an epidural rather than a general anesthetic, I could eat, but my excitement precluded enjoying breakfast, and after a few nibbles, I pushed the tray away. Bryan returned to my room, and we sat holding hands until two orderlies arrived, wheeling a gurney.

They positioned it so I could sit on it, and an orderly lifted my feet as I lay down. Bryan followed us down the hall, to a large operating room, all shiny clean, with masked people putting things in place. The whole event had been choreographed, and the medical people knew what they had to do and where they were supposed to be.

I saw Bryan had changed into his hospital greens, and he sat on a stool to the left of my head. He wasn't going to coach me through this birth as he had with our daughter's but I was glad he'd be near.

A sheet was fastened across me, hanging down onto my upper chest. My family doctor had come, and she stood behind the anesthetist, who sat on a stool to my right. He introduced himself to Bryan and me, and started setting up the IV line. My doctor smiled at me reassuringly. I'd been with her for six years, and I was glad she'd been able to come to observe the birth.

The anesthetist explained that they would go slowly when giving me the anesthetic. I wondered why, but then I remembered the form I'd filled out. I'd gone into cardiac arrest once before while being put under, but I'd hastened to explain that I'd been unconscious at the time. Still, I reasoned, they wouldn't want to take any chances. Then it occurred to me that if they were going slowly, maybe they'd start the operation too soon.

I turned my head and said, "Don't start the operation until the epidural has taken effect."

"Don't worry," the anesthetist said, patting my arm. "We've already started."

The drugs to relax me, as well as the epidural, did their magic. I was quite dozy for the birth of my babies. I found out later that the operation had started at 11:00 a.m., and the first baby had been removed fourteen minutes later. One of the nurses had promised she would call out what the sex was, and I heard her saying, "It's a boy." As each baby was lifted out, a nurse with a blanket rushed him to the NICU, to the neonatologists and incubators.

As each baby was delivered, the nurse called out, "It's a boy." When the last baby was delivered at 11:16, she said "It's a boy too," and I noted the surprise in her voice. The nurses had thought he would be a girl because his heartbeat had been slower. In two minutes, we had become a family of seven. Two minutes to seven!

Once I knew my babies were alive, I fixated on having my tubes tied. Bryan and I had told the doctor when we'd first arrived at the hospital, that I wanted the procedure. She was hesitant to agree, because I was still young, only thirty-three years old, but after Bryan and I explained our rationale, she accepted our decision.

We maintained that as long as one of the babies survived, we would be grateful. If none survived, we didn't think we'd chance another pregnancy, and risk conceiving multiples again.

"Don't forget to tie my tubes." I said from the operating table, unaware if anyone was listening. I dozed again, and missed the rest of the conversation, but Bryan didn't. The next day he told me.

"After the first baby was delivered," he said, "I knew I wasn't going to faint, and I stood to get a better view. The surgeon reached in—it seemed under your ribs—to get another baby. When the third baby came out, he was held upside down and he urinated onto the doctor."

Bryan laughed at the memory. "When I saw that I thought to myself, '*That's* my son!'"

The birth had gone well, and the attending physicians were in a good mood. One of the doctors heard me reminding them to tie my tubes, and asked Bryan, "Do you want us to do just one?"

"Everyone's a comic," my husband replied.

As planned, after the cesarean, I was taken through the NICU to look at my babies, my sons. I couldn't see much. Inside each incubator was a scrawny, tiny, humanoid form–a head, a torso, arms, legs. Baby D had quite a bit of black hair, but there were patches shaved off so electrodes could be attached. I had been prepared for the sight of them, but I still marveled at their small size.

Each baby had a tiny respirator attached to his mouth. After I saw each boy was alive, and receiving the medical attention he needed, I was glad to be taken to the recovery room. I was given Demerol, a very weak painkiller that made me sleepy, but I was glad to have time to recuperate.

As I drifted in and out of conscious awareness, I worried about Baby D, who had been the biggest. Floating around my head was the thought that in a multiple birth, the bigger multiples often don't fare as well as their smaller siblings do.

"Poor Baby D," I thought.

The next day, I discovered Baby B, the second biggest, had also had problems with fluid in one of his lungs. Both of them could have had a ruptured lung, but fortunately, it didn't get that serious.

Our hometown paper had their story ready to print, and as soon as they received word from the hospital, they ran it with headlines screaming, "THEY'RE ALL BOYS!"

When Bryan phoned our friends in Peterborough, after he'd had lunch, he was surprised to discover they already knew. Several other Canadian papers also carried the story, albeit in smaller print, and not on the front page. An announcement of the birth also made the TV news in Toronto and our hometown.

Two days later, when I was feeling stronger, my parents brought my darling daughter to the hospital to see me and our babies. I was very happy to see her, but sitting in a wheelchair as I was, found it difficult to hug her. She was shy at first, but was soon walking beside the chair, hanging onto my arm.

I wanted to reassure her of my love. I'd written her a few letters while I'd been having the non-stress tests and ultrasounds, reminding her that Daddy and I loved her, even though we had to be apart. After her initial wariness, she seemed happy and content; maybe she realized our separation was nearly over.

Bryan and I took my parents and our daughter to the NICU. Meggie was disappointed she couldn't hold a baby, because she had a cold, and she had to look through the window into the unit. Granny Jean and Grandpa Tony opted to do that as well. Bryan and I donned gowns so we could enter the NICU, and point out which incubators held our sons.

My parents took Meggie back to London with them after a short visit. As glad as I was to see my daughter, I could only tolerate a brief visit. After hugs all around and an extra kiss for my sweet daughter, I bade them goodbye.

Bryan and I spent the rest of the week at the hospital. He shared some of the medical information he'd picked up, talking to technicians and nurses. Our sons were being given a hormone to close the patent ductus, an artery that allows blood to bypass the lungs when a baby is in utero.

This drug didn't work for Geoffrey, Baby D, and it was the first bad news we'd received. His lungs weren't clearing, which meant his oxygen levels couldn't be reduced. This led to him losing weight, until he was the lightest of the four.

At the beginning of October, the doctors would decide to operate, to tie the tube off surgically. This would leave a scar under his arm that would grow with him, eventually stretching from his front to his back. However, it was a life-saving operation, and immediately after it, his lungs cleared. The nurses were able to start lowering the oxygen level, and he quickly regained the lost weight.

I paid short visits to my babies, during that week and I noticed they had patchy scalps. To check their oxygen levels, blood samples were being taken regularly. So much blood was used that the babies needed transfusions. When the doctors needed a new intravenous site, they chose a blood vessel in each baby's scalp, causing a little more of their birth hair to fall out.

I was disappointed that I couldn't breastfeed my sons as I had my daughter. I had held her to my breast, on the delivery table, immediately after her birth. Instead, I had to use an electric pump. I spent twenty or thirty minutes, four times a day, connected to it.

Each baby received milk via a thin tube, going through his mouth into his stomach. A small syringe was connected to the tube. The nurse held it five inches above the baby's mouth, allowing the liquid to flow in by force of gravity.

Before feeding a baby, however, the nurse had to check for fluid in the stomach. If a large amount of aspirate was left, it meant the baby hadn't tolerated the previous feeding. A careful check was kept not only on the amount of food being given, but also on how well it was tolerated, before the amount was increased. My husband the engineer was interested in such things. Volume in and volume out--it was right up his alley!

Two Minutes to Seven

While at the NICU checking on our sons, my husband also discovered that the boys were being given physiotherapy. When he returned to my room, after I'd rested or finished with the breast pump, he described what he'd learned. Since the babies were ten weeks premature, they had not developed a coughing reflex to clear their lungs of fluid.

The therapy consisted of the nurse using a small plastic cover (it looked like a miniature toilet plunger without the handle), to strike the baby over his lungs, loosening any mucus that had accumulated. This she drew out with a syringe.

The medical intervention keeping our sons alive was intriguing, but I wanted to settle the questions of names. Calling them Baby A, Baby B, Baby C and Baby D was getting tiresome.

During the summer, Bryan and I had thought about possible names. But since we hadn't known the sex of each, we'd come up with one and a half pairs of boy names we liked, and one and a half pairs of girl names. We'd given Meghan two names–Irene, Bryan's mother's name, being her second.

After having been presented with four boys, we had to make adjustments. Paul Bryan was one pairing we'd decided on. Alan was the other name, and John as a second name came after a bit of thought.

Deciding on the two remaining names took several days. Bryan mentioned names he liked, and I stated ones I liked. One or two names I wanted were rejected by Bryan because they reminded him of people he hadn't liked. I was more concerned about having initials that looked good and didn't spell anything obvious.

We both liked the name Richard for another son. After a couple of days, we decided on Owen as Richard's second name, but it took several more days for us to decide on Geoffrey Todd's name.

54

Bryan wrote each name on a piece of paper and pinned it to the incubator. When we went in to see that baby, we debated whether the name was suitable. It was hard to tell their personalities, of course, since they were so small and still. For that week, the hospital personnel had to use letters to refer to them. One nurse said she didn't like doing that.

Justifying our actions, Bryan said, "The boys are going to have to live with these names for a lifetime. It's better to take time to decide and choose wisely."

Some of our friends came up with their own suggestions for names, ranging from the ridiculous, "Eeny, Meeney, Miney, and Mo" to the religious, "Matthew, Mark, Luke and John" to Rock 'n' Roll, "John, Paul, George and Ringo".

As the week drew to a close, Bryan and I knew we'd have to face the media. Bryan and the hospital had been protecting me thus far. The hospital had handled all publicity through the PR department, and Bryan had screened phone calls coming to my room.

As we prepared to leave the hospital, the PR department arranged a press conference. I sat and smiled while Bryan answered questions, handling the reporters with aplomb.

"Bryan, what will you do with four sixteen-year-olds wanting to learn to drive?" asked one reporter.

"I'll buy four 1980 cars. They will be delivered in several buckets. I'll tell them if they want to drive them, they'll have to fix them," said Bryan with a smile.

We left Toronto and drove home, glad to be getting back to married life. I was very happy to be returning to my city, my house, my bed. I also wanted my former life, but it was not to be.

6: How to Eat an Elephant

My bed in my room in my house--the setting was familiar, but my life was not. This time, however, my memories were clear and I knew what was happening.

I was no longer only Meg's Mum; I was now a mother of five, and I only had a short time to adjust before my whole family would be living with me. It had never been easy for me to accept change, even without the brain injury. How would I cope now?

My husband also had to cope with the increase in our family, but I knew better than to try to change his routine. He still had a job to go to, and he wanted to escape and be out of the house early. After a fifteen minute walk to work, he could get a cup of coffee and regain his humanity. I arose to kiss him before he went downstairs and a few minutes later heard the door close as he left the house.

"Hi Sammy. Hi Stace." I greeted the cats as I walked down the stairs, alone in the house. I had to make my own pot of tea—no hospital personnel to cater to my needs.

I sat in the brown swivel rocker, given to us by Bryan's co-workers, while I had my own caffeine fix, enjoying the view from the picture window in the family room. It was a very comfortable place to sit while I was connected to the breast pump.

The hospital had given us small bags to collect the milk. We sealed the full bags and stored them in the freezer until we went to visit the babies on the weekend.

And Babies Make Seven

I heard a knock on the back door, and heaved myself out of the chair. I was still walking carefully, although nothing really hurt. I opened the door to a public health nurse, the one who had visited me during the summer.

"Welcome home. You must be relieved the birth went well."

"Yes, I'm glad that's over, but now the real fun will start."

I led her into the family room.

"I've arranged for a homemaker to come each weekday from 9 a.m. to 1 p.m.," she said. "I see the breast pump has been delivered."

"Yes, thanks." I didn't want to ask how the homemaker was being paid for, but I knew Bryan and I couldn't afford the service. I discovered later that community agencies had stepped in to cover the cost. "I'll start contacting the four friends who said they'd lend us a crib, so we'll have them here by the time the babies come home." I added, wondering if I sounded as tired as I felt. Even phoning people would take enormous effort.

"Good. And you'll have help getting Meggie to nursery school, until you're feeling well enough to do it on your own?"

"Yes. Ladies from the church have offered to do that. After Mom and Dad bring her home this afternoon, I'll phone the woman who offered to coordinate the volunteer help, and she'll arrange it."

When I had first discovered I was carrying quadruplets, I had told the priest at the Anglican Church I attended. He, in turn, had announced to the congregation what our situation was. Many people had offered to help, both before the babies came home and afterwards as well.

"It sounds like you've got things under control. I'll come back in a couple of days."

"Thanks. I'll see you then."

57

How to Eat an Elephant

She left. I didn't feel like I had things under control. So many tasks, so little energy. What should I do? I lay down to rest. This became my preferred way of dealing with stress and it worked, for the time being.

When my parents and daughter arrived two hours later, I greeted them warmly. I was very glad to have my daughter at home, to be able to re-establish her schedule as quickly as possible.

She had been Bryan's and my whole life for three years, but had lived with her grandparents for the past six weeks. Short visits, a few phone calls, and several letters had been her only contact with Bryan and me. Now, before the babies came home, we would have time to focus our attention on her once again.

My parents left the next day, and our life returned to some semblance of order. The homemaker came every morning. She did light housekeeping tasks, and helped to amuse my three-year-old daughter. Even with that extra help though, I often struggled.

I was on an emotional roller coaster. People who visited me were happy and excited, and I joined them in being thrilled to have a large family. However, when I was on my own, my mind swirled around thoughts of four cribs, sheets, blankets, and baby care items. Added to the vortex were household chores, cooking and cleaning. And…I had to spend time with Meggie. And…I had to sit for twenty minutes, four times a day, connected to the breast pump.

Many days, I felt swamped. One night I finally admitted to Bryan that I was overwhelmed, and could not cope. My spirit lifter told me the story of eating an elephant.

"You don't eat an elephant all at once," he said. "You just eat it one bite at a time. We'll handle our lives the same way. Parishioners are bringing dinners to us, and on the days they don't, I'm able to do the cooking. The public health nurse, the homemaker and many volunteers are coming to help. We'll manage."

"I guess so," I replied.

As the days progressed, and I got stronger, I found that we *were* managing. Friends and neighbours popped in or phoned, and my natural good-humour began to return. A couple of weeks later, I wrote to my mother: "having the homemaker here each morning sets me up for the rest of the day."

When the homemaker arrived at 9:00 a.m., I was usually sitting in the brown chair, connected to the breast pump. By the time she left at 1:00 p.m., my daughter and I had had our lunch, and the volunteer had arrived to take her to nursery school. Meggie had switched from going in the morning, to the afternoon, at the beginning of the school year.

I rested while she was away, and a short time after the volunteer brought her back from school, Bryan arrived home. Different parishioners brought our dinner to the house on Monday to Thursday nights. Bryan only had to cook on Fridays and the weekends.

For the month of September, Bryan took Meggie to her friend's house on Friday after we'd eaten. That meant we had only ourselves to think of each Saturday when we traveled to visit our sons. We arose at 8:00 a.m., ate breakfast and left.

When we arrived at the hospital two hours later, our first task was to hand the thermal bag containing the frozen breast milk to a ward nurse so she could label it and put it in the freezer. Then we gowned and went into the nursery.

We spent the day at the hospital, watching our sons, looking at the machines that kept them alive, and talking to the nurses who cared for them. On our second trip, we were very excited to be able to hold Paul, the smallest of our sons.

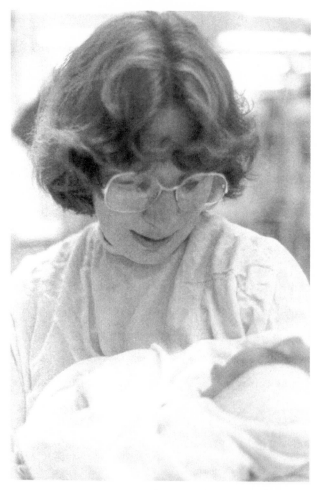

Figure 3: Valerie and Paul

"Here's your son, Mrs. Keelan." The nurse handed me blankets wrapped around a tiny pink face.

"Thank you." I murmured softly, not wanting to waken him.

Five months had passed since we had first learned I was carrying quadruplets, and finally I was able to hold one of my babies. I smiled at the tiny face. I couldn't really cuddle him because there was no weight to the blankets, and I couldn't feel where he was.

Secretly I was relieved he was too small to come home. How would I have cared for him? It was still several weeks before he should have been born. His ears weren't even formed.

Because he was weightless, I was afraid of crushing him if I tried to move. I smiled at Bryan, standing a few feet away, setting up to take a picture. I waited until Bryan put the camera on the floor and approached, before making a move.

"Here," I said, extending my arms. "It feels like blankets with nothing inside."

He accepted the bundle. "Wow, you're right. Can you take a picture of me?"

We traded places, and I snapped his picture. I put the camera on the floor and stood beside the chair. We stared at our son, scarcely believing how tiny he was.

After ten minutes, the nurse put him back in the incubator, after fastening some material over his eyes.

"This prevents UV rays from damaging his eyes," she explained.

Bryan took a picture of him and then proceeded to the other incubators to take pictures of our other sons. It was fascinating to watch them, and simply observe the sleeping forms. Other than occasional arm and leg twitches, the only movement was the slight rise and fall of their chests. They were alive, and they were ours.

My husband wanted to record our sons' journey, from incubator to home, on film.

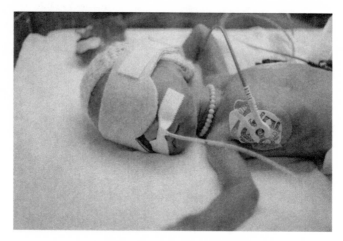

Figure 4: Paul in his shades

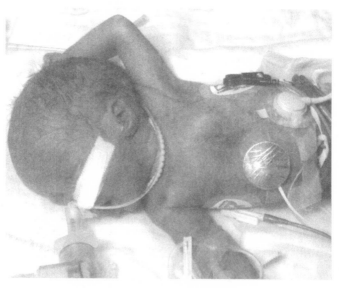

Figure 5: Alan

At the time, I didn't pay much attention. After a few years, however, I was able to sit and enjoy looking at the pictures. That was when I really appreciated Bryan's photography—when I could delight in viewing snapshots of my sons without worrying about their health and future.

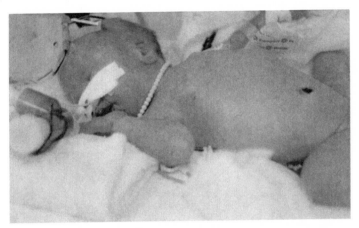

Figure 6: Richard

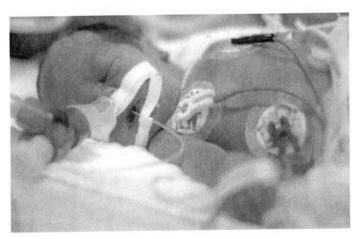

Figure 7: Geoffrey

However, in the days when we still had cause for concern, we ate in the cafeteria, and talked about our sons. It was too early to get a sense of who looked like which side of the family. We couldn't even tell if they looked like our daughter, at that age! All we cared about was that even though they were small, they were pink and healthy.

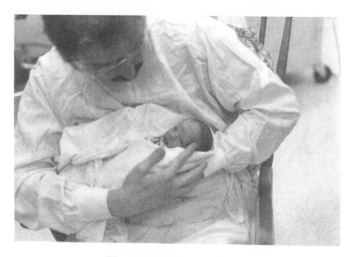

Figure 8: Bryan and Alan

After lunch, Bryan put his arm around my shoulders as we looked at our babies through the window of the NICU.

"It's over, Val. We've done it! Well, the first stage, anyway."

"Yes. So much anticipation and here we are! I wonder what'll happen now." We stood in silent contemplation for a minute, and then walked out of the hospital, arm in arm.

We had crossed the first hurdle, but what about the days, weeks, months, years ahead? Like Scarlett in Gone with the Wind, I couldn't think about that now. I had to take one day at a time. I was glad Bryan didn't mind driving. It gave me a much-needed chance to rest. Back in Peterborough, we picked up our daughter before returning to the house.

The next weekend, on our visit to the hospital, we were able to hold Alan, who was breathing well enough on his own to be removed from the respirator. Once again, it felt like I was holding nothing, just a pile of material. But when I looked at my arms, there was a tiny baby face almost hidden in the blanket.

We continued our weekend hospital visits for that month. Bryan phoned the hospital every day to check on our sons and he charted their weight and growth. I was glad he did that, and I knew he would tell me if anything was amiss, but I had more than enough to contend with at home.

Several weeks after returning home, Bryan, Meggie and I traveled back to Women's College Hospital to attend a babies' shower.

We walked into the foyer of the hospital, decorated with bunches of five balloons. The four blue ones and one pink one, tied together, represented our four new sons and our daughter.

One table held gifts. On another was a large cake decorated by students in a catering program of a local community college. Two large bulletin boards, placed to one side of the room, displayed pictures of our sons and the doctors and nurses who had helped at their birth.

Gazing around, I realized that the hospital had put much effort into the reception. I knew that our sons were only the third set of quadruplets born at the hospital in its 75-year history. This was a few years after the infant deaths at Toronto's Sick Kids hospital, and a time when hospitals were happy to have good news to report. Bryan and I were delighted to let Women's College Hospital have the positive publicity.

The hospital had sent out announcements of the boys' birth to various businesses, asking for donations. We felt most fortunate that one company undertook to supply us with formula in ready-to-use bottles plus disposable nipples, for the six months that the boys needed it. We also received baby creams, baby powder, baby soap, and other supplies to keep babies smelling and looking good.

Several TV stations had sent reporters to the event. Bryan and I had become accustomed to handling the media, but I felt sorry for my daughter. I knew she was shy, as I'd been at her age, and she wouldn't enjoy having a large microphone held in her face. Reporters asked her how it felt to have four new baby brothers, but how could she answer a question like that? She just smiled and looked cute, letting her pink T-shirt proclaiming, I'm A Big Sister, speak for her.

Figure 9: Meghan, the Big Sister

When the party was over, and we'd loaded all the loot, as Bryan called it, into the car for the ride home. I was exhausted. Our daughter was tired as well and we both rested on the trip home, leaving the driving in Bryan's capable hands.

And Babies Make Seven

At the beginning of October, Alan and Paul, who had been off their respirators for a couple of weeks, were deemed fit enough to be transferred to our local hospital. They arrived on a Saturday, which meant that Bryan, Meggie and I were at the hospital to greet them.

I watched as orderlies rolled the incubator off the elevator into the hall. A newspaper photographer was snapping pictures of the two babies inside it and of Meggie as she peered at her brothers.

"My babies!" she exclaimed, clapping her hands. She walked beside the incubator, making happy little noises. Bryan and I, the proud and happy parents, followed.

As the nurses took over with our babies, we talked to the newspaper reporter. The questions were similar to the ones we'd answered when the boys were born. I let Bryan do the talking: yes, we were happy. No, we hadn't expected a multiple birth.

I went into the nursery. The doctor, who was going to be an important part of my sons' lives for the next few years, extended his hand in greeting. We shook hands and introduced ourselves. A few minutes later, my husband entered.

"Bryan, this is the doctor who will be the boys' pediatrician." They shook hands. The doctor was busy and after another quick peek at our sons, Bryan and I left.

The next day, I tried breast-feeding Alan, but my heart wasn't in it. There was excitement in the air. I felt I should be doing something, not just sitting in a chair in the hospital room, nursing my son.

Alan was fussing. He was used to drinking from a tiny bottle, which required less effort. I could've persevered, and continued holding him to my breast until he learned how to nurse, but I didn't.

How to Eat an Elephant

I did keep pumping my breast milk, and we continued our weekend visits to Geoffrey and Richard who were still at the hospital in Toronto. Alan and Paul were put on formula, and as Bryan and I visited them and watched them grow, we felt we'd made the right decision.

By the beginning of November, which was the boys' due date had they gone full term, Alan and Paul were ready to come home. The other two were ready to be transferred to our community hospital.

Bryan and I wanted the transfers to happen at the same time because we didn't want to have to go to Toronto while we had two newborns at home. Our wishes were granted, and Richard and Geoffrey came to Peterborough a week after Alan and Paul came home.

The homecoming was another media event. A TV crew from the local CBC station came to our house, and while the reporter was talking to Bryan and me, Meggie stood on the couch beside Bryan and mussed his hair. I let Bryan do the talking, smiling and nodding at his comments.

One day we had two television crews, one from Peterborough and one from Toronto, in the house at the same time. While one was talking to Bryan in the downstairs nursery, I was showing the other the upstairs nursery. Maybe it was a slow news day in the big city!

I had only one week to get used to the new arrangement when our situation changed again. Richard came home. Bryan and I now had three babies, a three year old, and two cats living with us.

Geoffrey had developed a condition called 'bronchial-pulmonary dysplasia', and was put on low-flow oxygen. He could have come home as well, but we were reluctant to do so. It was complicated enough, with our family and the extra helpers. Having him at home, attached to an oxygen tank that needed to be turned down incrementally each week, was more than I could deal with. It was enough, knowing my son was only a short drive away.

Because of all the media attention, people were aware we'd had a sudden increase in our family. Friends, family members, and even strangers, sent us cards. One sunny afternoon, I opened a card to discover it contained a $20 bill.

My daughter was sitting at the table beside me and, seeing the bill, she said, "Is this dollar for me, Mum?"

"No," I said.

"Who's it for?" She asked.

"Mum and Dad."

She stood on the chair and clapped her hands. "I have a good idea. We can share it, Mum and Meggie and Dad." She was delighted.

"No Meggie, it's just for Mum and Dad."

My daughter was crestfallen. She sat down again, put her chin in her hands with her elbows on the table, and said in a soft voice, "I was really happy when I thought it could be for all of us, Mum and Dad and Meggie, but now I'm really sad."

I turned to her and gave her a quick hug. We'd used the cash we'd been given to buy the van, and to pay for live-in help, but we were still short of money.

"Oh Meggie, I'm sorry." But inside I was laughing. What a ham!

Her life was topsy-turvy, but Bryan and I thought she was adapting well to the arrival of her brothers. We were fortunate that many visitors brought a present for her when they came with presents for the babies. The three of us had had a month together while the boys were at the hospital in Toronto. Still, she had to find her own way to make sense of her new world.

How to Eat an Elephant

Another time, she suggested to me that "those of us who have lived here the longest" could go out, and "someone else could look after the babies."

In spite of this seeming disinterest in her brothers, our daughter had a connection to them that Bryan and I didn't. She was able to tell them apart by their cries when they first came home from the hospital. For those first two years when I had so much volunteer help, I constantly confused them.

Our family was being reunited, but it was happening in stages: first Alan and Paul came home, and then Richard did. Geoffrey was in the Peterborough hospital. Bryan and I could finally see all our children together.

This happened the first weekend in December. We used our van to take the other three babies and Meggie to visit Geoffrey who was now on the pediatric floor. Bryan carried Richard, in his car seat, and left him beside Geoff, who was in another baby seat in the crib. I waited in the van with Meggie and the other two babies. When he returned, we carried Alan and Paul in their car seats while Meggie trailed behind.

We placed the remaining two baby seats in the crib--four babies, in two rows facing each other, all in Geoff's crib.

"Wow." I thought. "Look at that!"

"Val, can you step to one side, please?" Bryan was preparing to take a picture, and didn't want my arm in the shot.

I stood out of the way, marveling at the fact that no one was crying. Geoff, with the oxygen tube crossing his cheeks, looked perplexed at the intruders. Meggie, sitting among the boys, looked pensive. What was she going to do with all these brothers?

It really was awe-inspiring! It was easier to acknowledge that I had been involved in one of the worst car accidents in Canadian history, than to accept that I had given birth to natural quadruplets.

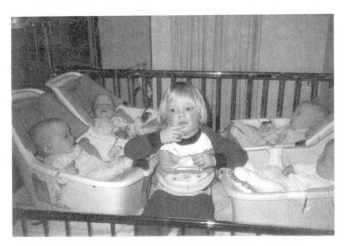

Figure 10: What will I do with all these brothers?

But I had, and our family now included seven people. Bryan and I were responsible for the other five. How had we come to be in this predicament? Sure we had wanted children, but five of them in three years? Were unplanned events, coincidences if you will, going to be de rigueur for our married life as it had been for our meeting and courtship?

7: A Rebel and a Seer

Bryan and I had met each other during the summer of 1978 through circumstances that could only be described as coincidental. If I hadn't been in Bala that summer...or if I hadn't phoned my girlfriend...or if Bryan hadn't moved from Saskatoon...if, if, if...but many unplanned events had shaped my life to then, and even my parents' life before I was born.

My parents had met on a blind date. Dad had been serving in the Royal Netherlands Army in Southern Holland in 1940, when Hitler had overrun the neutral country. He had managed to escape and had ended up in England. Plans were being made to set up a recruiting centre in Canada, in Stratford, Ontario, and when one soldier couldn't go at the last minute because of illness, my father had volunteered to go.

When my mother was 18, she and her family lived in Stratford. She was in her final year of high school in January 1941, when the soldiers arrived. That September, one of her friends was going to the Fall Fair with a Dutch soldier, and she told Mom: "I'll ask him to bring a friend." That blind date led to my parent's courtship.

Mom and Dad celebrated their first wedding anniversary in August 1943. Dad was sent to England the next month. As a member of the Dutch Army, he went into Holland in May 1945, after it was liberated. Mom sailed to Amsterdam in October, to join him, and her parents sponsored both of them to immigrate to Canada the next year.

They settled in Stratford, where Dad worked as a bookkeeper at a factory. A few years later, they moved to London Ontario, and while working at another factory, Dad studied to become a Certified General Accountant. My older brother had been born in Stratford, and I was born in London. In 1954, when I was two and my older brother was four, we moved to Huntsville in Muskoka, Ontario, where Dad set up his own accounting business. My younger brother was born two years later.

Dad's office was in the Town Hall, the same building as the public library. When I was old enough to go to the library on my own, I stopped in to visit, especially when my mother was working there, which she did during income tax time, March and April.

Figure 11: Val (age 3) and Steve

A Rebel and a Seer

My mother was involved in the community as a member of the Association for the Mentally Retarded (now called Community Living). She also taught children's dance lessons, and I attended.

Mom and Dad didn't have a perfect marriage. They argued frequently, but as a child, I felt loved and secure. Our family life during my growing-up years was a positive influence on my decision to have children after I was married.

Living in a small Ontario town in the 1950's and 1960's was agreeable. My brothers and I could walk to a candy store to spend a penny or nickel. We lived a ten-minute walk from the school. I accelerated through grades three, four and five in two years. Because of that, I was always younger than many of my classmates. I didn't mind, as a young child. In my teens, however, I was attracted to boys who were a year or two behind me in school.

My brothers and I had many cousins. My mother was one of four children and my father had a sister. Two of my mother's siblings had five children each. In later years, I was to use those aunts as role models, rather than my own mother.

I did pattern myself after my parents in my religious life, however. We attended the Anglican Church every Sunday. I joined the choir and a girls group as well as going to Sunday school. Church activities were part of my life, and I was happy.

As well as being an accountant, Dad also helped the priest, taking summer church services in the area. He decided to pursue further training as a lay reader, and it was during that time he felt a calling to ordained ministry. Moving away from Huntsville in the summer of 1966, which at the time seemed to be just another stage of growing up, was actually a turning point in my life.

74

And Babies Make Seven

Dad was sent to be the rector of St. Paul's Manitowaning on the Manitoulin Island. It was a three-point parish, which meant he was also responsible for two other country churches.

St. Paul's, the oldest Anglican parish church in Northern Ontario, was in the back yard of our house. The church had been built in 1835 for the island's native population. Guidebooks list it as having "three beautiful stained glass windows" above the altar. The windows, which depict the Risen Christ in the centre window, St. Paul offering the mission church in Manitowaning in the left window, and an Indian offering a sheaf of corn in the right-hand window, were installed while Dad was rector.

Surrounding the church was an old, unused graveyard, with gravestones dating back to the 1860s. The first summer we lived there, my brothers and I walked among the gravestones, taking note of the names and dates. Watching my older brother mow the lawn, I knew he was glad the stones had been laid flat in the ground.

The Anglican rectory was a four-bedroom, square wooden house with a small, enclosed front porch. Our tap water came from a cistern in the basement, and every weekend my brothers had to drag a hose to the creamery next door to fill the cistern.

My mother did not like the idea of our water being stored in a large open reservoir in the basement, and the next year, a permanent pipe was installed, connecting our house to our neighbour's water line. The village didn't have a public water system until 1975.

While living in Huntsville, I had been an accountant's daughter, but after our move, I was part of a rectory family. This accorded me a certain status. Dad expected my brothers and me to go to church every Sunday, and his parishioners likely assumed the three of us would behave better than other teens. However, I often told my friends that I was the

75

still the same person, no matter what my father did, and if I wanted to say 'shit' or 'damn,' I would.

I thought of myself as a rebel, even if no one else did. The summer of 1967, I rolled out of bed at the sound of the church bell ringing at 8:25 a.m. I pulled a sweatshirt and pants on, over my pyjamas, ran a comb through my long, naturally curly blond hair, slipped a pair of runners on, and rushed out the back door to the church. I was obeying my father's wishes, but on my own terms. At the end of the service, I left quickly. By the time Mom arrived home, I was back in bed and asleep.

Two years later, I was 16 and worked as a telephone operator for the summer. The village didn't have dial phones until the 1970s. When we'd moved, our phone had been an old-fashioned one, with a separate ear- and mouthpiece. Shortly thereafter, we switched to a regular rotary phone, but we were on a party line for several months.

I had no premonition that my summer job as an operator was not going to be the first of many. I did not believe in fortune telling, the occult or any kind of magic.

If I had, I might have paid more attention to a feeling I had had when I was nine or ten years old, and still living in Huntsville. I began to think that I did not want to be nineteen. I was afraid that something bad would happen to me. My plan to deal with it was to say I was eighteen for two years, and then turn twenty. Even if that had worked, it would not have prevented the tragedy. I had miscalculated by two years and I was seventeen when tragedy struck, in 1970.

8: Loss and Rebirth

The events leading up to that year began at the New Year's Eve dance in the town's Orange Hall, in 1968 when I met a boy who had recently moved in with his grandparents across the street from the Anglican rectory. We began dating.

We only saw each other on the weekends during the school year because the village didn't have a high school. My parents had chosen to send me to Espanola High School the year before, when I was in grade eleven. Having started at that school, I continued to go to it the next year, even though a high school had been built that year, on the Island.

Two of my girlfriends went to the school in Espanola as well. We boarded there during the week, and made the Friday afternoon and Sunday evening journeys, one hour each way, together.

My boyfriend was in grade ten at the secondary school on the Manitoulin Island. The summer that I worked as the telephone operator, he worked on the ferry crossing from South Baymouth, on the Island, to Tobermory, on the Bruce Peninsula.

One Saturday afternoon, I was upstairs in my bedroom, getting into my bathing suit and combing my hair when I heard a knock at the front door.

"That'll be Paul." I called down to my mother. "We're going swimming with Sharon and Brian." I slipped a long T-shirt on, grabbed my towel and ran down the stairs.

"Where's Paul?"

"He's waiting outside. I said you wouldn't be long."

"Thanks, Mom. See you later. Bye."

I was out the door before she replied.

Paul was standing under the tree in our front yard. We joined hands and walked to the main street, talking about 'These Eyes' a new song by The Guess Who. The main street was deserted. We walked past the restaurant and the bank, and crossed the street at the corner.

We continued down the hill, on the path through the underbrush and came out at the end of the road that wound down the hill to the wharf. Our friends were already there.

Manitowaning Bay is part of Lake Huron and the water at the wharf is sixteen feet deep. We jumped in or dove off the main dock and swam to the smaller dock then swam back. We spread our towels on the dock, protecting us from the gravel, since cars also drove there.

Other days, if we didn't want to swim, Paul and I walked to the Dairy Queen for a cone, after work. Occasionally we went to Paul's place to listen to records. He had every Beach Boys' album and most of the Guess Who as well.

When school started in September, I again traveled to Espanola each Sunday night and returned every Friday afternoon. My friends at school knew I was dating Paul and they teased me, "Val's favourite expression is 'How many days to the weekend?'"

During our time together, we talked about his plans for the future. He wanted to become a musician and start a band. Then he would be able to move away from Manitowaning, which didn't have happy memories for him. He and his five siblings had been separated a couple of years previously when his mother had died, following his dad's death. He and his younger brother had been sent to live with his dad's parents.

And Babies Make Seven

Paul and I went to the New Year's Eve Dance again in 1969, to celebrate our one-year anniversary. It came as a complete shock, therefore, when he suggested, the next month, that we break up. I was totally unprepared for it and was devastated.

One sunny day I went for a walk. The snow was shiny white. I thought about walking forever, and not having to cope with what was happening. I didn't want to try to figure out why Paul wanted to break up. I walked several miles out of town before going into a farmhouse and phoning for a ride home. My parents and brother had searched everywhere, including the shoreline, trying to find me.

February and March were difficult months. When I was at home on the weekends, I was in a constant state of teenage angst, but when I was at school during the week, I was a typical grade thirteen student.

At the end of March, my life changed irrevocably.

*   *   *

When my mother told me what had happened, I didn't know if I could believe her.

God grant me the serenity to accept the things I cannot change. Car accidents were not something that happened to me. I usually read about such things in the newspaper. And when she told me that six of my friends had died, I was very confused. That certainly was not something that happened to me.

Courage to change the things I can. But what had happened? I thought I remembered being at a hospital and getting into an ambulance. And here I was, lying in a hospital bed, unable to bend my legs, unable to feed myself, unable to smile, unable to cry. I could talk, but slowly with much effort and in a monotone, and I yawned constantly. Why was I here? I tried to remember.

Loss and Rebirth

And Wisdom to know the difference. I couldn't ask anyone. Whom could I trust? Was I asleep and dreaming, or had I been before and was I awake now? How could I know? I thought I remembered being normal... I thought I remembered... I didn't know...

Serenity, courage and wisdom—I needed all three in my present circumstances. Why was that prayer running through my mind? My mother told me that she had recited it to me while I was unconscious. It had been imprinted in my psyche, but it did not answer the question uppermost in my mind: was I dreaming?

"Pinch yourself to see if you're awake." Why did I think that? If it was true, it might be the answer to my question.

My midriff became inexplicably (to my parents) black and blue. But it didn't help me. Sometimes I could feel it and sometimes I could not. I didn't realize that my brain injury had lessened my sense of touch on the right side of my body.

A friend gave me a travel alarm clock to keep by my bed, and I watched it to see if the hands moved. Lying by myself in the hospital bed, they didn't seem to, but when I had visitors, they did. What did that mean? I was confused but complacent, bewildered but accepting.

My friends came to visit me and as they talked about what had happened two months previously, (a couple of yesterdays in my mind) my memory began to solidify, and the dream about the ambulance ride faded. Six friends didn't come to visit me. Maybe they really were dead.

My parents wanted to take me home, to let me live in familiar surroundings while I adjusted to my new reality. The doctors agreed. I was taking valium but otherwise wasn't receiving medical care.

Our house had to be rearranged to accommodate me. I was not able to climb stairs to my second floor bedroom, and so my bed was moved downstairs to the dining room. We had to rent a commode chair since there wasn't a bathroom on the main floor.

My mother took me off the tranquilizer. I hadn't been agitated since regaining consciousness, but with my mother there to calm me if needed, drugs weren't necessary. I gradually came to accept my new life, but how different it was!

I had to be pushed in a wheelchair. I had progressed from eating strained food to eating mushy food before I left the hospital, and at home, I started to eat proper food. I was also getting better at feeding myself.

As my strength increased, I began to walk around the house. At first I had to hold onto my brother, mother or father, but as my confidence increased and my balance improved I was able to walk alone, touching the furniture or walls to steady myself.

As I learned to accept my new life, I also discovered what had happened during the two months I'd been comatose. The accident had occurred on the Saturday night of Easter weekend. My friends and I had been driving to a dance, but my father hadn't wanted me to go. My mother had argued that since I'd be going to university the next year, it was time to let me make my own decision.

I never blamed my mother for the fact that I was in the car that night, since I probably would have gone without parental permission. I had been very upset after breaking up with my boyfriend, and that night I was going out with another boy.

The doctor who responded to the emergency call hadn't thought I'd survive the trip to the hospital. Since there were only two ambulances available, I travelled to the hospital in the back of a station wagon.

After a couple of weeks, when I'd shown no sign of regaining consciousness, the doctor had decided to operate on my legs. I was given a general anesthetic, which was standard procedure at the time to ensure that I didn't move during the operation. My legs, which had been in traction since the night of the crash, were removed from the constraints. A pin was inserted into the bone of my right leg, making a cast unnecessary.

The next day, however, as I was being put under to have the second operation, I went into cardiac arrest. It took the doctor and nurses twenty minutes to get my heart beating properly again. This threw everybody into such a tizzy, that all plans to fix that leg were abandoned.

I was oblivious to the drama surrounding me. I did not know that the doctor had to decide whether it was better to try to fix my leg, and risk death from the anesthetic, or not do anything and ensure that I would be crippled for the rest of my life. He considered the dilemma for a week, and during that time, my leg was not in traction, and it started to heal.

The doctor decided to operate, but to use a local anesthetic. Because the bone had started to grow together, he had to break it again and piece it together around the pin. When I woke up, it was virtually the same length as my other leg, but if I was required to stand for any length of time my legs hurt, and I attributed this to the fact that the main bone in each had been broken. However, much later in my life, I discovered that the main reason for the pain was that my left leg was turned and the muscles, tendons and ligaments were twisted.

When I was fifty, the arthritis in my left knee became so painful that I had to have knee replacement surgery. During the operation, the surgeon was able to turn my leg before attaching the new knee, and afterwards, I was able to stand relatively pain free. In the 1970s, however, I sat as often as I could, and was thankful that my leg worked at all.

My older brother visited me in the first few weeks after the accident. He held my hand, and asked me questions, telling me to 'squeeze once for yes and twice for no,' and apparently I answered one or two questions correctly, but I have no memory of doing so.

Six weeks after returning home, I was admitted to the Ontario Crippled Children's Centre (now the Bloorview Kids Rehab) in Toronto, where I received physical, occupational and speech therapies.

One aspect of my physical therapy was to push an occupied wheelchair. I asked my visitors to sit in the chair, to provide stability, while I pushed them. One friend of my parents, a physical fitness buff, found this most embarrassing.

"Are you sure this is what I have to do?" He'd ask. "Can't I push you instead?"

"No." I'd reply. "I have to push you."

Occupational therapy included dressing myself and doing my hair. The nurses were amazed to discover I could stand in front of a mirror and braid my hair in two side braids. I'd been doing it for ten years, and it didn't seem remarkable to me.

I had always been able to talk, after becoming conscious, but my speech was very laborious. Thoughts formed in my head readily enough, but it took effort to verbalize them. I practiced tongue twisters to increase the speed of my speech. Exaggerating tone variation as I talked eventually enabled me to speak in something other than a monotone.

At the Centre, I took psychological and IQ tests to determine the extent of my brain injury. They revealed my intellect was intact, which was a great relief to my parents. It came as no surprise to me, since I felt the same, inside my head. It was only when I tried to express myself that I was frustrated.

The physical aspects of my recovery progressed steadily. I concentrated on that aspect of my recovery since physical independence was essential to being able to live on my own. The emotional part of my recovery didn't seem as important. I never regained the ability to shed tears. Not being able to express emotion has remained my biggest handicap, but over the years, I have learned to live with this, to accept that this is just the way I am.

9: A New Life

In December 1970, my father transferred to the small Anglican parish in Englehart, Ontario. My younger brother, who was in grade ten, and I moved with my parents. My older brother was attending university, and no longer lived at home.

The son of the former priest still lived and worked there. He was my age, and since I was unable to walk outside by myself, he accompanied me. Mom offered him a cup of coffee when we returned, after having been outside for an hour or more in subzero weather. My top speed, which kept me warm, was a saunter for him.

Most days my father and I walked to the post office. He escorted me, nodding to people in passing. I kept my eyes down, watching my feet. Dad checked our mailbox and dropped letters in the mail slot. One day in February 1971, however, we had to forgo our morning walk.

"Mom," I called up the stairs in my peculiar sounding voice. "I have to mail a letter. Can you come with me?"

"Just a minute," my mother called from the upstairs bedroom where she was sewing. "I'm almost finished."

I waited, and called again. The same answer. I waited what seemed like forever and tried again. The same answer.

"Mom will never come," I thought to myself. I looked out the window. It was a bright day, but no new snow had fallen.

I already had my boots on. After slipping into my coat, putting my hat on my head, and pulling on my mitts, I grabbed my letter, opened the door and stepped onto the porch. I was in trouble already--from the porch to the sidewalk were three steps, but nothing no railing to hold onto.

I looked to the right, to the church and its parking lot--no one there. I looked to the left. More houses, but no people. If anybody had been within hailing distance, I would have called someone over.

Without assistance, there was only one way I felt safe. I squatted down and sat on the top step. I bumped down the few steps and stood on the sidewalk.

"I can do this," I thought. The post office was only half a block away. It was strange, walking without hanging onto someone's arm, but I did it all the time in the house. Why should walking outside be any different? Lift my heel and push off with my toe. Bend my knee, raise my leg and bring my foot forward. As that heel landed, I bent my foot and shifted my weight forward. That would bring my heel on the other foot up, and I would be ready to start the process again. I had to concentrate to keep my feet as close together as possible. Otherwise I would look like I either "had to go or had just gone," as my older brother lovingly joked.

I had put the letter in the mail slot, and was returning home when I met a neighbour.

"Hi Val, does your mother know you're out alone?"

I shook my head. I couldn't stop to talk. I had to concentrate on keeping my balance. When I got back to the house, I had to crawl up the steps onto the porch. As I raised myself to my feet, I saw my mother standing at the door.

"Oh Val, there you are! I suddenly realized you weren't calling me, and I wondered where you were."

Later, telling my dad what had happened, she said, "Val walked like a drunk, trying hard not to stagger."

Figure 12: Val and Barb, 1971

For the next month, when I went walking with my friend, I let go of his arm for progressively longer periods, until I was able to walk alone. What freedom that was! I could go out whenever I wanted. Sometimes I went out by myself simply because I could.

Learning to walk outdoors by myself was the last hurdle preventing me from pursuing my education. By the fall of 1971, I was ready to attend school again. My doctor suggested I try something easier than university, which is where I had planned to go the year before.

Since North Bay was only a two-hour drive away, I decided to enroll in the home economics program of its community college. I took courses dealing with food preparation and nutrition as well courses to do with patterns and making clothes. I completed my first year of study, with good grades.

By this time, I had gotten glasses to correct my double vision. The prescription was complex since I needed a prism to help bring what I saw from each eye into a single image. Wearing glasses corrected most of my vision problems, but I became used to a shifting view, since the refocusing mechanism in my eyes had been damaged, and briefly, every time I blinked, the images split and rejoined.

Although my walking was slow, at least I no longer walked like a two-year-old. My voice, incorporating the natural rise and fall of inflection, didn't sound as strange. I was returning to normal!

The summer of 1972, I lived in Bala with my grandparents. My five boy cousins, who also lived there, and with whom I had shared many happy childhood summers took me in as a sister. My boyfriend and I broke up, but I handled the split better. He went his way and I went mine. When I saw him a few years later, I discovered he had gotten married.

I graduated from the two-year college program with a diploma in arts & science, rather than home economics because I was not able to complete a sewing course. My ability to do such an activity was hampered by my vision problems, and the shakiness in my arms.

After I graduated from college, I moved to Bala again, and spent the summer with my grandparents. In the fall, I moved to Bracebridge. I worked for friends of my parents, looking after the woman's mother who was crippled with arthritis and could not be left on her own. I had tried a real job, working at a Kentucky Fried Chicken store, and had had to quit because I experienced pain being on my feet for an eight-hour shift.

And Babies Make Seven

I applied to Guelph University, and started in January 1974, studying psychology. After attending three semesters in a row, I transferred to Waterloo University. The psychology program had involved taking a course in statistics, and because of my double vision, I couldn't keep the figures straight. I switched to Human Relations and Counseling Studies, which didn't require a statistics course.

My friend Barb, whom I'd known for twenty years, was also attending Waterloo University, and that was another factor affecting my decision to make the move.

One Saturday evening, I knocked on her apartment door.

"Hi Barb," I said as she opened the door. She was a single mother, and her young sons hid behind her.

"Hi Val, come in. I just have to get these two into bed."

Barb and I didn't visit often, both being busy with our studies. We rewarded our hard work with an occasional wine and cheese evening. She joined me in the kitchen, after settling her sons. She prepared the cheese and retrieved the wine from the fridge, while I got two goblets from the cupboard.

We talked about essays and papers, and other aspects of university life. After a while, our conversation moved to other matters.

"Do you remember I told you about the dream I had when I was becoming conscious?" I asked.

"Yes, weren't you afraid of being buried alive because you thought no one realized you weren't dead?"

"Yes, I was going to walk across the hall to ask my mother to waken me. My legs couldn't support me because I'd been in bed for nearly two months, and when I tried to stand, I just collapsed.

"But later I did walk even though I was unconscious. My mother gave me a chalkboard to use while I was in the hospital, and I remember writing 'the doctor says I can go home' and 'I can walk'. The nurses decided to humour me. I walked with a male nurse on either side of me, and another nurse on her hands and knees, moving my feet, but I don't remember any of it."

"What's that like?" Barb said. "Not being able to remember those two months?"

"Life continued around me, even though I wasn't taking part in it. In that way, it's like I died and came back to life. But it's also as if I was asleep for two months, because I had a dream at the end. Because of the experience, I feel comfortable talking about death; it doesn't scare me."

"It must be hard living with the fact that you survived and your friends didn't."

"I missed the tragedy because I was unconscious, but I can't ever forget what happened. Every time I move or talk, I remember that I'm not the same. While I used to be a 'normal' teenager," I said, sketching the quotation marks in the air with my fingers. "Now I'm like this. Sometimes it bothers me, but I believe God is looking after me."

We talked a bit for a bit longer, but it was late. We said good night, and I left.

Walking home, my thoughts returned to our evening's discussion. Another fascinating question was, "Is there life after death?" If I hadn't woken up in this world, I would've been in another state, i.e. dead. In that case, I wouldn't be able to ponder the question, would I? Are dead people aware they are dead? Even though I had been close to death, I was no closer to the answers. Mulling the question over, as I walked home, didn't bring any fresh insights.

I let myself into the house where I boarded. Before getting into bed, I set my alarm clock, so I could attend church. Even without my father's dictum, I still attended regularly.

I went to church Sunday morning, and in the following weeks and months, Barb and I spent a few more evenings together. They were interspersed with all-nighters to finish projects and essays. Such is the life of most university students.

By June 1975, I had been attending university for over a year. I felt I deserved a break, and planned a train trip to the West Coast. I could afford both the trip and my university education because of the insurance settlement I'd been awarded.

It had been a messy court case. Sixteen people had been involved; eight in each car, and both drivers had been killed. Between 1971 and 1973, I went to several examinations of discovery. I was interviewed by numerous lawyers. My parents drove me to Toronto for the sessions.

One time, my mother and I went into an ornate washroom before entering the boardroom. Looking in the mirror after washing my hands, I flicked my hair this way and that.

"Aren't you nervous, Val?" my mother asked.

"No, I can't answer any questions. I don't remember anything from twenty-four hours before the crash until two months after."

"You don't remember Terry asking you to go to the dance?"

"All I know is what you've told me: He asked me, and we went with Ann and Boyne, who was driving."

"And you don't remember giving Paul, Hugh, Wayne and Marty a ride?"

"No, I only know they were hitchhiking because you told me."

91

A New Life

We left the washroom and entered another room. I sat at a long oak table with my parents on either side of me, across from the lawyers and clerks. I gazed at the shelves lining the walls, filled with books I couldn't hope to read.

One lawyer asked me how I was different from what I'd been before the accident. I pulled a face and looked at my mother.

"It's hard to remember what Val was like before," said my mother. "It's not something you usually notice. You don't normally think you'll be quizzed on it. She was a typical teenager. She liked to skate and ride her bike, but she can't do either of those things now. And she always did well at school. She's finished high school because her teachers gave her a passing grade based on her work in the first two-thirds of the year. She didn't go back to school after the end of March.

"She was an Ontario Scholar," Mom added.

"That means she got over 80%, right?" said one of the lawyers.

"Yes."

I had been seventeen when I was injured. I was still growing and maturing. I didn't care about my personality development. I could talk; I could walk. I was continuing to improve. I was getting on with my life. Later I did wonder whether muted emotions and a calmer demeanor actually helped in the raising of five children, but since I hadn't known that was to happen, any discussion of my personality seemed irrelevant.

Rather than being concerned with personality changes, I focused on my physical abilities. I stumbled occasionally, especially if I turned around too quickly. I had to hold a railing if I went up or down stairs. I couldn't have passed a sobriety test, not being able to put one foot in front of the other. I had to walk with a wide stance. I couldn't touch my nose with my finger, and trying to pat my head and rub my stomach elicited gales of laughter from me and whoever was watching.

This preoccupation with physical prowess led to my wish to learn to water-ski. My cousins skied every summer, but I had never tried it.

In the early 1970s, however, I was trying to shed the label of being disabled. I had gone from sitting in a wheelchair to pushing one, to walking while holding on to someone, to finally being able to walk on my own. I was eager to prove that I was normal. Learning to water-ski at the age of twenty-one was one way to do that.

When I told my cousin Don what I wanted to do, he offered his aid, and enlisted his brother Paul and friend Steve to help as well.

One Saturday in July, Steve drove his family's yellow motorboat, with Paul along as lookout. Don was treading water and holding my skis straight while I sat in the water, my life jacket keeping me afloat. I remembered my preparatory talk with Don, sitting on the dock.

"I'll be in the water with you. You hang onto the rope, and as it gets tight, I'll give the signal to Paul and he'll tell Steve. The boat will speed up, and if you lean back, it'll pull you out of the water."

I saw the rope uncoiling in front of me. I noticed Don swimming out of the way and raising his arm. Paul turned his head, and the boat took off. I leaned back. I tried to hold my legs together. I tried...I tried...but I couldn't. When I hit the water, I got water up my nose, before remembering to let go of the rope. Don swam over to me.

"Are you all right, Val?" Don was concerned, but as I was laughing and sputtering, he smiled too.

"Yes, I'm fine," I said pushing my hair off my forehead, and wiping my eyes. Don swam towards shore and I followed. We sat on the dock, watching the guys retrieve the skis.

"Do you want to try again?" Don asked.

"Yes!"

"This time I'll sit in the water with my arms encircling you, I'll have skis on too, and will be holding a second rope."

Figure 13: My waterskiing crew, relaxing after success

I was supposed to get up with Don's help, after which he would let go of his rope, but I couldn't do it, and we both fell.

"I wonder if we should try having you sit on the dock for the takeoff," said Don when we were back on shore.

"Thanks, Don, but I'll wait for a bit, I think."

I smiled at him as I turned and went up to the house. As I entered through the back door, remembering to dip my feet in the bucket of water to remove the sand first, I met my grandmother in the kitchen.

"I don't know why you want to do that, Val. Your poor legs, after all they've been through."

"I don't know either, Granny, but I do. We'll try later. Don will think of another way."

"I'm sure he will, dear." Granny said, shaking her head. But I knew that secretly she, and probably Grandpa too, thought I was foolish to try.

'Waiting a bit' turned out to be the next year.

"Let's try having you sit on the dock, Val. Hold the rope, and when it gets tight, just stand, and the boat will pull you."

"Sure, Don. Where will you be?"

"I'll be in the water at the end of the dock, ready to help if needed."

I sat on the dock, waiting for the rope to tighten and pull me up, but it didn't happen. I was pulled off the dock, but it wasn't to stand and ski, it was to fall and be dragged through the water.

My cousin's next plan was to have me sitting on the bow of a canoe, while he paddled. Since I was already partially standing, it should've been easy to pull me into a proper skiing stance, but it wasn't. Whether it was lack of coordination or a balance problem was unknown. All that was improving was my ability to let go of the rope quickly.

"Next year," I said to Don, wrapped in my towel and back on the dock after our failed attempt. "I am going to do this, no matter what!"

"Yes, we will do it," said Don, laughing. "I'm taking it as a personal challenge as well. I *will* do it. It'll just take the right technique."

It was two summers later before we were able to have a weekend at Bennochy, as my grandparents called their house, to try again. By then my legs were strong enough, and my balance had improved sufficiently that I was able to get up from a water start. Don met me at the dock, after I'd completed my circuit.

"I watched you shifting your weight from one leg to the other, trying to keep your balance, and I thought for sure you'd take a tumble, but you held on."

A New Life

"Thanks Don. I wouldn't have done it if you hadn't kept trying too. We both deserve credit for this!"

Having achieved my goal, I was content. I have never felt the urge to skim the surface of water again. Having proved to myself that I could do it, I had accomplished my goal.

I accomplished another of my goals that year, when I graduated from university with a General BA in Human Relations and Counseling Studies. I knew having that particular degree wouldn't prepare me for a job, and I had always assumed I'd get another. Little did I know that my education thus far, the BA and the diploma from community college, would equip me to deal with my life far more than I could have imagined.

Since I was unemployed in the summer of 1978, I moved to Bala to work for my grandparents. I helped Granny around the house, and I was able to drive Grandpa's car if he didn't feel like going out.

Driving a car was another process that had been interrupted in 1970. I had gotten my driver's license in 1969 after having turned sixteen in December of the previous year, but I had let it expire when I was injured. By 1975, when I was living in Waterloo attending university, I wanted to get my driver's license again.

I had trouble getting my beginner's license because of the eye exam, but after getting a note from my ophthalmologist, I was ready.

People who knew what I'd been through, however, didn't trust me to drive their car. How was I going to practice to pass the driving test?

One friend, who hadn't known me before 1970, saw me as a fully capable young woman. He lent me his car, a station wagon without power steering. I had to parallel park it, but I passed the test.

And Babies Make Seven

While living with my grandparents that summer of 1978, I was able to drive my grandmother to a meeting if my grandfather didn't feel like going out--little things that made their life easier.

"I couldn't manage without you," Granny often said. I was pleased, but at times, I was also bored and unhappy. I wrote in my journal, "I seem to be busy all the time, but I don't accomplish a lot." How many times was I to express that same sentiment after I became a wife and mother!

Other than my cousins, who were working at summer jobs, I didn't know anyone my age in the area. In a phone call to my mother one day, I learned that a girl I'd gone to elementary school with was staying at her grandparent's place in Bracebridge, a mere thirty-minute drive away. I phoned to see if she was interested in getting together.

She suggested I go to her place that Saturday for lunch. Driving the country roads in my black Chevette, I wondered about the wisdom of this decision. We had been good friends in school, but that had been twelve years ago. What would she think of me now? Would I even recognize her? I remembered she'd had long, brown hair that she'd worn in one or two braids.

Having found her house, I parked the car and got out. I recognized her immediately, although she'd cut her hair, and I remembered her younger sister who was also there. There was a boy there, Bryan, and I was unsure whether he was her boyfriend, her sister's friend, or a neighbour.

She introduced us, saying he was 'just a friend.' He may've been just friend to her, but he was to become much more than that to me.

10: Magic and Mechanics

It was serendipitous, the way Bryan and I met, and a blind date had brought my parents together. It wasn't surprising, therefore, to learn that a chance encounter on a bus had led to Bryan's parents becoming acquainted.

The Second World War had been the catalyst in my parents' meeting, and I discovered the same was true for his parents. We discussed how our parents had met, one day while we walked in the park.

Bryan's dad, Gerry, was an RCMP officer in Saskatchewan in the late 1930s. The Canadian army had agreed to send military police officers overseas to honour its commitment to the war effort, and the RCMP volunteered the personnel. Gerry was sent to England and was stationed to Aldershot, Hampshire, as part of the Canadian Provost Corps in the 21st Army Group.

Bryan's mother, Irene, had attended high school in Newbury, Berkshire, England before deciding to become a teacher. She attended a Teacher Training College, and after completing her course, accepted a temporary teaching post in her hometown. She spent a year there before taking a permanent job, teaching eight-to-ten-year old children a general course, or what was commonly called the 3 R's, (reading, writing and arithmetic) in the Aldershot area.

After their meeting, Bryan's parents pursued their relationship at the canteen where Irene volunteered in the evenings, and after a brief courtship, they married. A daughter was born in 1944. The three of them moved back to Saskatchewan, Canada the next year when Gerry's assignment ended. Bryan's brother and another sister were born in Regina. In 1952, the Keelan family moved back to England, taking a transatlantic voyage on the 'Empress of France.' They settled in Bradfield, Berkshire, eighty kilometres west of London.

This low-lying land adjacent to the River Pang was ideal for Irene to cultivate a large garden of vegetables and flowers. At the back of it, she kept chickens, which provided eggs for the family of five. The house had a climbing rose along the front and sides, thanks to Irene's green thumb.

As we walked and talked, and with pride in his voice, Bryan told me that his dad had worked in London as a liaison officer, in conjunction with Interpol and the British police. He was with Security and Intelligence, the surveillance arm of the RCMP (now CSIS). One of his tasks was to do Visa control, security screening on new immigrants who wanted to come to Canada.

Bryan related the family lore about his birth. Apparently, Irene was told she *couldn't* have any more children when the doctor meant she *shouldn't* have any more children. This lack of communication led to Bryan's premature birth in April 1953. He weighed only three pounds–a harbinger of his sons to come, perhaps?

He wasn't expected to live, and because his father was Roman Catholic, he was baptized in the hospital. Defying the odds, however, he thrived.

When his oldest sister pushed him in a pram as his mother pushed the other two children in another one, people stopped the nine-year old girl to look at her "baby," expecting to see a doll. They were shocked to see a live infant!

Magic and Mechanics

Across the road from the Keelan house, which was named Rouen according to local custom, was a forge where a blacksmith and his assistant shoed horses and did other ironwork. The blacksmith had learned his trade before the use of tractors, when horses performed the work on a farm.

Bryan recounted how, as a four-year-old, he had ridden his chain-driven tricycle over to watch the men effortlessly swing hammers, transforming a red-hot iron bar into a uniquely shaped horseshoe, which was nailed to the horse's hoof.

One day his tricycle stopped working, and Bryan couldn't understand why. He dragged it across the road to show his friend, the old blacksmith, who did something to it, and magically it worked again.

Bryan could not comprehend how the blacksmith had fixed his trike, but he had been so impressed that telling me about it, he added, "I thought it was magic, seeing him fix my tricycle back then. That sense of wonderment still echoes when broken things are made whole, even now."

After he told me, I wondered if the experience had also been the reason he had decided to become an engineer. Certainly, given our family life that was to come, he would have many opportunities for the magic to echo as he worked on computers and bicycles for our children. But he wasn't to know that then...

Bryan talked about his living arrangements as a child. He and his siblings bathed in a metal bathtub, and a coal stove in the kitchen heated their house. They didn't have a TV set, and he had to go to his friend's house to watch his favourite show, The Lone Ranger. In place of a clothes washing machine, they used a copper, which was a pot where the laundry was boiled every week. Unlike many of their neighbours, they did have a large fridge, which his father had bought from an American soldier who was returning to the States.

When the Keelans moved back to Canada in 1958, they sailed on the SS Homeric. Bryan showed me a picture of their family seated at a dining table during the crossing. At age four, he was a real cutie, with dimples and a big smile. The trip took five or six days, and they landed in Montreal.

From there they took a train to Winnipeg where his dad's mother and two sisters lived, as well as their brother with his family. Bryan and his family lived in Winnipeg for several years before his dad retired from the RCMP.

Figure 14: Bryan, age 6

Magic and Mechanics

He was pensioned off in 1962, and joined the Saskatoon city police as a civilian employee, running the Central Records.

When Bryan had started school in Winnipeg, he was teased because he spoke with an English accent. By the time he and his family moved to Saskatoon, however, he was in grade four and had lost the accent. It was only noticeable when he became upset. Those situations arose occasionally as he walked to school. To get to the Roman Catholic school he had to pass a public one, and in those days, the kids going to the different schools often fought. He was taunted and had to dodge the occasional rock thrown his way, but he didn't fight back.

When his father had married his mother, who was an Anglican, she had had to sign a paper saying she would raise her children as Roman Catholics. This was a common practice in Canadian Society at that time. Bryan and his siblings jokingly called his mother a 'black protestant.' She took it in good fun, but attended an Anglican service on her own when she wanted to go to church.

Bryan's parents, like mine, didn't have a perfect marriage. His mother hated the snow, cold and long winters on the prairies, and she especially missed the spring flowers for which England is noted. His father drank more than he should have, to cope with the pressures of his job, but he didn't physically abuse his family. While there might not have been money for extravagances, there was always enough to put food on the table. He also didn't stop his wife from listening to Gilbert & Sullivan operas, which were her favourites, and which Bryan came to love as well.

By 1970, Irene began having problems with her back, and as the pain forced her to do less and less, her children had to do more and more. Bryan's task was to do the laundry. The back pain was diagnosed as bone cancer in her spine and although she lived six months longer than was expected, she died in August 1971. Bryan had just finished high school.

He hadn't been prepared for his mother to die. In fact, he had had no inkling that she was even close to death. This was before the time of grief counselors, and the Keelan family, like many in that situation, didn't have professional help in dealing with the loss.

Bryan coped with his grief by immersing himself in life at the University of Saskatchewan. He also tried to pretend nothing had happened. Since he was the only one still living at home, he felt responsible for helping his dad manage. In many ways, Bryan ran the household while his father drank more heavily.

His dad liked to go to the local Legion. After Irene's death, Gerry spent even more time there. He befriended a woman who worked there, someone he'd known for several years, and they decided to marry in 1972, which Bryan felt prevented his dad from drinking himself to death. His stepmother's children were mostly married and living away from home, but she did have a sixteen-year-old daughter, who was still in high school. Bryan was happy to be part of a family again.

In September 1971, he began attending the University of Saskatchewan, studying electrical engineering. During his fourth year, he signed up for an interview with CGE (Canadian General Electric, now GE Canada) because they were at the top of the list of prospective employers. He wanted experience in taking an interview in order to make a better impression for a later job he might really want. However, the interviewers from CGE offered him a job in Fuel Handling. He took it with the intention of moving to Ontario for a year or two, to see how the Easterners lived.

Magic and Mechanics

He left his home in Saskatoon, in early June 1975, driving a 1959 Jag. He drove east and east and east, then south and south and south, and was amazed to discover he was in what the locals referred to as 'northern Ontario.'

"They don't know what north is," he thought.

Although CGE was in Peterborough, he learned when he checked in at their headquarters in downtown Toronto that he was going to be on a graduate engineer-training program in Hamilton. Since he was unused to the traffic of Southern Ontario, he had a map handy as he navigated his route from Toronto to Hamilton. He was pleased to find his way to the correct highway, and was happy to be leaving the city before rush hour.

When he didn't see Hamilton on any of the sign postings, he became concerned. The map had indicated it was quite near. When he saw signs for Kingston instead, he pulled into a gas station, and consulted the map. He was dismayed to discover he was traveling in the wrong direction! Turning around to re-trace his steps he found himself in the stop-and-go traffic he had hoped to avoid.

Bryan worked in the CGE sales office in Hamilton for three months. He transferred back to the Peterborough location. After three more months, he was offered a chance of employment in Pinawa, north of Winnipeg, for a year.

While most people felt being that far north was tantamount to an exile, Bryan regarded it as a homecoming. He was happy to work as a research assistant at the Whiteshell Nuclear Research Establishment and when he relocated to Peterborough, in November 1976, he rented an apartment in a house. It was while living in this place that he met the girl who would turn out to be my former school chum.

And Babies Make Seven

In 1978, Bryan still found the heat and humidity of Southern Ontario unbearable. My former schoolmate's family owned a cottage on Lake Muskoka in Bracebridge, and she took pity on him, inviting him to visit for the occasional weekend. Since Bryan didn't know many people in Peterborough other than the people he worked with, most of whom were married, he was happy to accept her invitation. It was while on one of these humidity-escaping weekends that we met in June 1978.

*   *   *

After lunch Bryan, our friend and I went into town so I could shop for a bathing suit. He told me after we were married that he'd been disappointed I hadn't come out of the change room to show off the skimpy ones. The three of us swam and visited all afternoon.

Before I had left Bala that morning, my grandmother had suggested that after my visit I have dinner with my great-uncle before returning home. I asked my friend and Bryan to come with me, but she declined the invitation. Bryan accepted, and I phoned my great-uncle.

He chuckled when I explained my plans, but I'm not sure what he was more amused by–the fact that I was bringing a boy with me, or Granny's suggestion that I pick up Kentucky Fried Chicken and join him for supper. Bryan and I laugh about our first date now, involving as it did eating KFC and later watching Lawrence Welk on TV, neither of which we particularly liked.

Bryan wrote me three letters that summer, and we got together numerous times. Every time Bryan visited in Bracebridge, our friend invited me to go over. If she planned a trip to Peterborough, she phoned and invited me to go with her. The first time this occurred, I questioned whether Bryan would mind, but when she informed me that he'd asked her to invite me, I was happy to accompany her.

Magic and Mechanics

One trip was memorable. My cat lived with me at my grandparents' place, but they didn't like cats, and only tolerated her for my sake. I left her in a kennel while I was away for the first trip, but Bryan thought that was unfair to the cat and he urged me to bring her with me when I came again.

Bryan also had a cat, and the two felines, both older neutered females, didn't get along. When Bryan and I decided to go into Toronto to see his sister, during my second visit, I felt it necessary to take my cat with me rather than leaving her in a house with people she didn't know, and another animal she didn't like.

We'd been visiting for a couple of hours, when my cat squeezed through a hole, and became trapped between the tub-surround and the wall. Bryan could not pull her back out, but luckily, Rosemary's husband, another Brian, phoned from Calgary, where he was preparing for their upcoming move. He told Bryan there was a hole in the bathroom floor, and if he went into the basement, he should be able to coax the cat to come out that way. Bryan retrieved my cat in that manner, and we made it back to Peterborough without further incident.

The fall of 1978, with my cat living with my parents in their home near Windsor, I moved to my aunt and uncle's house in London and began attending another community college, training to be a library technician. Bryan was still living and working in Peterborough. We visited each weekend, with him making the trip to London one time and me making the trip to Peterborough the next.

Although we enjoyed being together, we hadn't thought seriously about a long-term commitment. When Bryan invited me to fly to Saskatoon with him to spend Christmas with his father and stepmother, I accepted, without thinking that this signaled a change in our friendship.

Although all of Bryan's friends that I met, and his family, saw this as a get to know you presentation tour, neither Bryan nor I saw it that way. We were just good friends who enjoyed each other's company.

As such, when I had to spend one week training as a library technician in the spring of 1979, I chose to work at a high school in Peterborough. I was able to stay with Bryan, who was sharing a house with two of his co-workers at CGE.

I didn't make a favourable impression at the school during my work term. Once again, my eyes let me down. I found it difficult to read the spines of shelved books, and I began to doubt that this was a good career choice. I did enjoy my week in Peterborough, and becoming better acquainted with Bryan and his friends.

By May of that year, I was half way through the two-year course. I was contemplating plans for the summer when my mother phoned to say there was a possibility of a job in Windsor: was I interested? I phoned Bryan to tell him.

"In Windsor?" Bryan exclaimed. "That's an awfully long way from Peterborough. We'll never be able to visit. Can't you get a job here?"

"I don't know how I can do that," I said.

Bryan replied, "What are we going to do?"

There was a pause. Then one of us, or maybe both, said, "We could get married."

We decided to do that although Bryan later joked that if he ever found out there wasn't really a job waiting for me in Windsor...!

I spent that summer in Peterborough, trying to earn money as a Fuller Brush salesperson. Selling was not my strong point, however. Believing that the product would sell itself, I didn't bother to learn anything about it. When a prospective customer asked me about a product, I looked it up in the catalogue, and read what was written. When a manager phoned to suggest I attend a workshop to improve my selling technique, I quit. I didn't make much money, but I had great cleaning products for several years.

My stint as a salesperson had ended in failure, as had my effort to become a library technician, but I didn't care. I was getting married! My mother, Bryan and I planned the wedding by phone, while I was living in Peterborough. Mom had had many chances over the years to observe what worked and what did not, attending weddings officiated by my father.

Bryan and I wanted our marriage ceremony to be a family affair and as informal as possible. We were happy to let my mother plan it, but we made the final decisions about the ceremony and reception, based on her suggestions.

It left us free to spend many hours together at the rented garage where Bryan stored his Jag. I talked to his feet and listened to him as he explained what he was doing underneath or inside the car. He was replacing the automatic transmission with a manual one. As we talked, I came to appreciate that cars were a big part of Bryan's life.

In 1974, he had been given a 1959 Mark III Jag with a 3.8 litre engine. One of his Dad's friends gave it to him on the condition that he fix it up and make it drivable again. He worked on it, and drove it to Toronto in June 1975. He also drove it in Pinewa the year he worked there. While driving to Saskatoon, after that job was finished, the car developed a problem with the wheel bearing and he parked it at his brother's house in that city. It had stayed there until he had it transported, on a trailer, to Ontario in 1978.

That summer, when we met, Bryan worked on the Jag as a hobby car. His driving car was a blue 1976 BMW, with a standard gearshift, which he had bought after borrowing a friend's for a day. He had been very impressed with how the Beamer had handled. Bryan taught me to drive it, and I came to love the cars as much as he did.

Bryan and I were both 26 years old, and we had known each other for less than a year when we married. We had similar outlooks on life, each being Pollyanna types who always tried to see the bright side of any situation. Our senses of humour were similar, leaning towards puns and word plays. We liked to go for long walks together, and being young and in love, held hands, which had the effect of slowing Bryan down to walk at my speed.

Although I did not consider myself a handicapped person, I did have limitations, which had prevented me from obtaining a job. Bryan had to consider this when we decided to get married. He knew that as an engineer, he would make a good salary—enough to support a wife and a couple of children. But, I'm sure he never anticipated married life with five children--a daughter and quadruplet sons.

11: Yikes! And This is Only Three

To be truthful, I hadn't imagined married life with five children either. I had assumed, growing up, that I'd have a child or two. After getting married, Bryan and I hadn't discussed the number of children we wanted. We thought we'd have a son and a daughter, but it was not to be.

Suddenly we had five children. By December 1986, four of them were at home and Geoffrey was only a ten-minute drive away, in the local hospital. Faced with reality, my husband and I donned our Pollyanna personas and plunged ahead.

Three babies enlivened our household and our three-year-old added her own unique vitality. My fellow parishioner, who was my volunteer coordinator, contacted women who were willing to help and she also organized their visits. Physiotherapists came to the house to work with the babies and visited our son in the hospital.

Our house resembled a train station, with people coming and going at all times. I often felt like I was between trains, or waiting for one to come in. This was my house, but much of the time, I felt like I'd gotten off at the wrong station. Luckily, others were on track.

The public health nurse arrived on appointed days, and on her advice, we put two borrowed cribs in a bedroom upstairs with two babies sleeping crosswise in one crib and the other baby sleeping the same way in the second, leaving a place to put the fourth baby.

The other two cribs were on the main floor, in the family room. Baby care items were stored in each place, giving us an upstairs nursery at night, and a downstairs one during the day. It was important for me to think we had a routine, but in truth, every day brought its own schedule.

If things were going well, I padded into the next bedroom at 6:00 a.m. to feed my sons. I lifted the lone baby in one crib, and placed him with his brothers in the other. I attached nipples to three bottles of ready-to-use formula, and propped a bottle on blankets, one for each baby. Then I stood back to watch, adjusting a bottle here, rearranging a blanket there. Like a maestro I was, with an orchestra of three.

Not every day was so serene. If I had been up during the night, which fortunately didn't happen often, I wouldn't be maestro, I'd be a parody of one. Imagine holding one baby to keep him quiet while trying to attach a nipple to two more bottles to feed the other two... Imagine two babies crying, and fumbling with the bottles and nipples while trying to keep them from waking my daughter... Imagine three babies crying, and... Imagine my husband, not a morning person, having to help me with the babies...

While I conducted my mini-symphony, on good days, Bryan was doing back up with Meggie. If she wasn't awake by the time he was ready to go downstairs, he woke her, and they ate breakfast as a duet. After eating and helping her to get dressed, his concert was finished and he left at 7:50 a.m. My musicians were resting.

"Meggie, do you want to sit with me and watch TV while I eat my cereal?" I asked.

"No," she said, running to the family room. She returned clutching a book. "Read this."

My daughter and I had been very close for the past three years. With our baby sons at home, and a host of volunteers coming into the house daily, I did not want her to feel neglected. I decided to forgo breakfast, and went into the family room with her.

Cuddled on the couch, we chuckled at the antics of the Berenstain Bears, with my daughter adding to the story, telling me of further pranks they might have played.

"Good story, Meggie." I stood, having heard the door in the kitchen open. "I think the homemaker is here now."

I looked through the doorway, and saw my lifesaver hanging her coat on the hook. Meggie ran to her. They greeted each other, and I knew my daughter would be happily occupied for the next couple of hours.

It gave me time to myself. I poured cereal into a bowl and added milk before sitting at the kitchen table. I thought about my children. We were very lucky that all the boys were healthy.

Geoffrey was in the hospital, but more as a convenience for us than because he needed medical care. I envisioned life with four newborn babies, a three year old, two cats and an oxygen tank, and shuddered. I would live with the stress of visiting my son in the hospital daily, until he was weaned off the oxygen. It was preferable to the anxiety the above scenario would have produced.

I put my dishes in the dishwasher and looked in the family room. The homemaker and Meggie were putting toys away.

"Thanks, Linda. I don't know how I'd manage without you."

"We're having fun, aren't we, Meggie?"

"Yes. Here comes another toy to jump into the box..." My daughter was actually enjoying tidying up!

I went up the back stairs to my bedroom. After getting dressed, I looked in on the boys. Three tiny humans, all breathing naturally, the deep rhythmic sounds of sleep. If it had been a chaotic morning, the sight of them sleeping erased that memory. I tiptoed out and went back downstairs.

The homemaker had made a pot of tea for me, and a hot chocolate for Meggie. While we sipped our drinks, Meggie practiced her animal sounds.

"What does a doggie say?" I asked.

"Bow-wow"

"What does a cat say?"

"Meow"

"What does a turtle say?" I asked, thinking to trick her.

"Turt-turt" said Meggie, never at a loss for an answer.

We heard a light rapping on the door, and Meggie ran over to open it. A woman from my church entered the room. She removed her coat and hung it on the hook. Then she traded her boots for slippers.

The volunteer, homemaker and I went upstairs, and each of us brought a baby downstairs. We sat in the family room. After feeding the babies, burping them and changing diapers, we settled them in the two cribs downstairs. The volunteer left.

The homemaker left at 1:00 p.m., as another two volunteers arrived. They stayed with the sleeping babies while I walked Meggie to nursery school. After returning to get the car, I drove to visit my son in the hospital.

As I entered the pediatric ward, I saw him in a baby seat, sitting on the desk at the nursing station. The nurses were working nearby.

"Hi Geoffrey," I called to him. "Are you keeping the nurses company?"

"Yes, he is," said one. "It's rather boring for him, sitting in his room all day, so we like to bring him out here."

"I'm glad you do."

I carried my son to his room and took him out of the seat. I sat and rocked him. He certainly was bigger than his brothers! His big brown eyes and chubby cheeks were reminiscent of a four-year-old Bryan sitting with his family on a ship crossing the Atlantic.

I put my finger in my son's hand to see if he would grab it. One time he closed his little fingers around it. I spoke softly to him, not really saying anything, but just letting him hear my voice. I wanted him to know that I was someone who cared about him, even though he only saw me two hours a day.

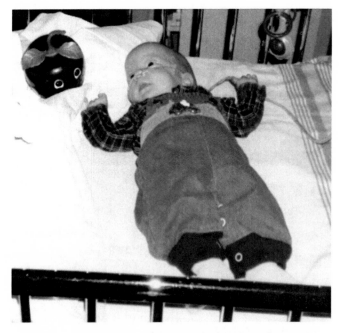

Figure 15: Geoffrey at the hospital in Peterborough

Another way to become acquainted, in the short time available, was to dress him in outfits I'd brought from home. Doing so gave me a chance to cuddle him. But I had another reason…

I snapped a picture of him in each outfit. The boys had been given sets of clothing, in similar or different colours. At home, we took pictures of the other three babies. Geoffrey would have outgrown the newborn size by the time he came home. In this way, we had pictures of all four babies dressed in similar outfits, even if the surroundings were different.

I carried Geoffrey up and down the hall. We sat and rocked in the chair in his room. All too soon, it was time to leave. After giving my son a final hug, I put him back in his crib. I left to get Meggie.

Figure 16: Richard, Alan and Paul

My daughter and I returned to the house in time for me to give one of the babies a bottle. The volunteers left after the babies had been fed and changed. With the babies in good spirits, lying in the cribs in the family room, and Meggie amused by a TV show, I was free to think about dinner. By the time Bryan arrived home, the food was nearly ready.

"What did you do today, Meggie?" asked Bryan as we sat at the table. In the background were (mostly) happy baby sounds, with the occasional squawk or squeal.

Meggie liked to tell a rambling story detailing her day. What happened on the TV show, Sesame Street, was often included.

"Sounds like you had fun." Bryan said, looking at me and raising his eyebrows. I shrugged, smiled and shook my head. I couldn't figure it out either.

At 7:00 p.m., it was time to feed the babies again. As I started to get three bottles ready from the stash we stored in the family room, I heard footsteps on the back porch, and a light rapping on the door.

"Come in," I called. Through the sheer curtain, I saw that it was my friend. After taking her coat and boots off, she followed me into the family room.

She picked Alan up and propped him on the couch beside her. I handed Paul to her, along with two bottles. She held him while she fed both babies. I took Richard out of the crib and sat in a chair to feed him.

When we finished feeding the boys, we changed their diapers and sleepers, and my friend left. She lived around the corner, and coming to help was her gift to celebrate the birth of my sons.

Meanwhile, Bryan had given Meggie a bath and read her a story. He tucked her in bed, and when I finished with the babies, I went in and kissed her goodnight.

One or two volunteers, people who didn't mind coming later at night, arrived for the last feeding at 10:00 p.m. Bryan might help at the beginning of the feeding, but he didn't like to be up too late. The volunteers and I finished feeding the boys, changed their diapers, and put them to bed at 11:30 p.m.

It didn't bother me that volunteers, people who enjoyed looking after wee ones, were coming into my house. All help was appreciated—it had been since 1970. Paraphrasing the Serenity Prayer, wisdom dictated I accept that which I could not change.

No, I did not want to change having people coming to help. My survival depended on them. Not just women from my church came to help. Others from the community were also eager to assist with the babies.

One such woman I had met the year before at the office of the Canadian Mental Health Association. (CMHA) I had discovered that the Peterborough branch of the CMHA needed a board member to edit their newsletter.

"I could do that," I thought. I felt a little over-awed saying I was on the board of the Mental Health Association, but as long as my only task was editing the newsletter, I could manage. Bryan supported me.

"What do you mean would I mind if you became a board member for CMHA?" Bryan asked. "It's up to you. If it's something you want to do, then go for it."

"I know, but I'd have to go to meetings once a month and I might be busy at other times, trying to get the newsletter out on time. That's all I'd be doing though, just the newsletter," I explained.

"You could do that. Now that we have a computer, I could show you how to use WordPerfect, and you could write it quite easily." Bryan was very proud of the computer he'd built.

Canadian General Electric, in a drive to get its employees computer literate, had offered a course that allowed staff to buy the parts to build their own computers.

"When I finish with this, Val," he said, "we'll either have a clone PC, or a $5000 boat anchor."

"Well, I hope we end up with a computer," I said, watching him attach the blue strap to ground him so no static electricity would fry the computer. Then he proceeded to solder more wires in place.

I had used a typewriter to write my newspaper columns. As soon as we had a computer, I wanted to be able to use it. However, the brain injury had reinforced my personality trait to wade into new waters cautiously. I was hesitant at first, but using a keyboard, whether on a typewriter or a computer, is the same and it wasn't long before I was composing, correcting and printing electronically.

I edited the CMHA newsletter for several months. After less than a year on the board, however, I had to resign. In accepting my letter of resignation, the president said, "This is the first time I've ever had to accept a resignation because the person was expecting quadruplets."

The woman who worked part-time in the CMHA office and I had become friends, and she phoned me in September.

"The sorority group I belong to undertakes to do good works in the community. At our meeting last night, we decided to help you and Bryan this year. We'll provide free baby-sitting, starting when your sons arrive home."

"Thank you. That's great!" I was surprised at the community support. "Will they be able to manage all the babies and Meggie too?"

She laughed. "We'll send two women at a time. They wouldn't do it any other way! Give me a call a day or two ahead of a planned outing, and I'll set it up."

"Okay." We hung up.

One day in December, I phoned her to arrange babysitters so Bryan and I could go to a twins club meeting. After we'd arranged that, she asked me how things were going.

"We took the kids to see Geoff at the hospital the other day. It was unbelievable-all five of them in one crib and four of them little babies!" I exclaimed.

"I know how special it is to have one baby. I can't imagine looking at four babies, knowing they're all yours. It is a lot of work, though. Which reminds me, what are you and Bryan planning for Christmas?"

She knew that Bryan and I liked to have a traditional turkey dinner at Christmas, and that Bryan always did the cooking.

I had recounted the story of my first attempt to cook a turkey, the year Bryan and I got married. I put it in the roasting pan with the legs on the bottom, and without a meat thermometer. When I took it out of the oven, it was an URT, according to Bryan, an Upside-down Raw Turkey. Thus began his tenure as turkey chef!

"We'll have a tree, and presents for Meggie like we always do, but there'll be no turkey dinner this year. Bryan will be too busy helping with the babies."

"That's what I thought," she said. "I'd like you, Bryan and the four children to come and share our Christmas dinner. My mother is visiting, and she'd love to see the babies."

Bryan and I accepted the invitation. In the remaining weeks before the holiday, I didn't notice the passage of time. My life was looking after three babies at home, visiting my son in the hospital, and caring for Meggie. It took nearly all my energy, but I did manage to accompany my daughter to a nursery school Christmas party.

Yikes! And This is Only Three

December 25 finally arrived, and Bryan and I wanted to visit our son in the hospital together. We noticed that nurses in the pediatric ward had pinned Christmas cards to a bulletin board to brighten the atmosphere. We took pictures of each other sitting in a rocking chair, holding our son. After the visit, we returned home and thanked the two volunteers who had given up part of their Christmas Day to stay with our other children.

In getting ready to go to our friends' house, Bryan let the van warm up, but we bundled the three babies in layers of clothing as well. Big mistake! When we got to our destination, they were hot and very upset. Fortunately, our friends understood the reason for the screaming.

Their teenage daughter took charge of Meggie. I took Richard out of his car seat, removed a layer of clothing and gave him to my friend's mom. She popped his soother in his mouth, and he quieted immediately. Bryan took Alan from his car seat and removed the extra clothing, and I did the same with Paul. With the babies calmed, we visited while my friend prepared the last of the meal.

Her mom asked how much the babies had weighed.

"Two eleven, two twelve, three four and three ten" I rhymed off. (1230g, 1250g, 1480g, 1660g) "Alan was the lightest, then Paul, and then Richard. Geoffrey was the heaviest."

"Three pounds ten ounces is not very heavy. It's amazing to think babies can be that small and survive," my friend said, turning to face us and waving a wooden spoon. "Okay, I think we're ready. Can the babies sit in their seats?"

We settled the boys, and sat at the table. The turkey dinner was delicious, and our daughter surprised us by tasting everything. After the main course, we broke open crackers, and wore funny hats while we ate pie and ice cream. After the meal, my friend, her mother and I sat in the living room to feed the babies.

"Did I hear you say you don't have overnight help any longer, Val?" My friend asked.

"Yes," I said. Then I felt I should explain, for her mother's benefit.

"One of Bryan's co-workers at GE knew a nineteen- year-old woman who came to live with us when the three babies came home. I handled it badly, though. She fed the three babies their middle of the night feeding, but I didn't insist she take time off during the day. After six weeks, she was burnt out, and had to leave."

"Are you managing on your own?"

"Yes. The babies sleep through most nights, and I learned how to feed them in their cribs, from our overnight helper. In the morning, the homemaker arrives shortly after Bryan leaves for work. I'm not left alone for too long."

"It must keep you busy, though."

"It sure does. That's why I'm glad to receive dinner invitations." I said and laughed.

We finished feeding the babies, and after burps all around, put them in their car seats. Bryan and I decided not to tempt fate. We thanked our friends again, said good-bye and loaded the kids into the van. On the drive home, I thought about our life, and the changes that were coming.

Bryan and I liked to visit friends in other cities. It would be more difficult to do that now. In fact, would anyone want us to, with five children in tow?

"What would a road trip with five children be like?" I wondered.

12: Everything is a Big Production

A chance to travel with the four children we had at home thus far came in January, when Bryan had to attend a work-related conference near the town where my parents lived. A trial run!

My friend and her daughter, with whom we'd shared Christmas dinner, came to help with preparations a few days before our journey. We washed and dried sleepers, receiving blankets, and undershirts and packed them in a suitcase. Check the sizes—medium for Richard, small for Alan and Paul. I counted and recounted, worrying that we'd need more. And diapers! Although I was trying a diaper service at home, I planned to use disposables for our trip.

"You're only going for three days, aren't you Val?" my friend asked, gently.

"Right. Let's see. Three babies, three days, three sleepers per day…how many is that?"

It was a lot. Twenty-seven. Maybe we'd need more! We took more sleepers off the shelving unit and stuffed them in the suitcase.

Six diapers per day per baby were fifty-four. Better take two boxes of forty-eight each. It was better to have too many than not enough.

Now, how was Meggie doing?

My daughter liked to pack for herself, but she needed supervision. I didn't care if she wore tops and bottoms that didn't match, but she had definite ideas about what colours went together, and what clothes she wanted to wear. She did have trouble thinking in terms of tops and bottoms. Arriving with four tops but no slacks wouldn't do! My friend's daughter had the patience to assist her.

That night, after supper, Bryan told me his plan for our trip.

"Five a.m.?" I squeaked. "I have to be ready to go at 5 a.m.? It'll mean getting up at 4:30."

"Yes, Val, but that way we can be on the road shortly after six, and we'll be through Toronto before we have to stop to feed the babies and change diapers." Bryan always tried for a logical approach to convince me of the correctness of his decision.

I appeared to give in to his logic, but I didn't really mind because I was a morning person. My balance was better, my double vision less irksome, and my tolerance for upheaval higher. Still, if I'd had to get up with the babies during the night …

Two days later, we were ready to go by our 6 a.m. deadline. With no middle of the night awakenings, I had gotten up at the appointed time. Bryan had only been awake for twenty minutes. We'd started this division of labour BC. (Before Children) He was able to get going more quickly than I, who wanted to leave the kitchen tidy and the bed made. I had been able to sleep in the car in earlier days, but that wasn't likely now.

Once Bryan was up from his extra lie-in, we took the children from cribs and bed. They weren't fully awake as we strapped them into their seats in the van. Meggie's booster seat sat on the first bench, with one baby seat beside it, and the other two infant seats fit on a bench at the back of the van.

In between the second and third benches was a table that doubled as a diaper changing area. The second bench, which could flip towards either the front or the table, was not sturdy enough to hold baby seats.

Everything is a Big Production

Since the car seats faced the back of the benches, I couldn't see the babies after they were strapped in. If someone on the bench at the back started crying, I had to get out of my seat and walk the length of the van, without disturbing Bryan, who was navigating traffic on the four-lane highway. As soon as I got to the babies, I quickly replaced a soother or adjusted a blanket and returned to my seat.

Sticking to our timetable, we made it to my parent's place before noon. Meggie ran to meet her grandparents as soon as Bryan took her out of her car seat. She remembered the computer games from previous visits.

"Donkey boom, G'andpa Tony, Donkey boom." She said, reaching up to grab his hand.

"Just a minute," he said as he bent to kiss her. "I have to help Mum and Dad with the babies first."

Bryan handed an occupied car seat to each of my parents. He took the third, and I took Meggie by the hand. We trooped into the house. Once inside my daughter started hopping from one foot to the other, chanting "Don-key-boom…don-key-boom….don-key-boom."

"Dad, why don't you take Meggie to the other room and play her game with her?" I suggested. "I'm sure Mom, Bryan and I can manage."

After they left, I handed Mom, sitting in a chair, and Bryan, sitting on the couch, a baby and bottle each. I took the third baby and bottle and sat beside Bryan. After we finished the feeding, Bryan collected the two playpens from the van. We set them in the living room and put Richard and Alan in one, and Paul in the other.

My mother looked at the clutter--blankets, baby coats, hats and booties--marking our progress from the front door to the kitchen to the living room. She shook her head, but refrained from commenting.

Soon after, Meggie and Grandpa returned and my daughter announced she was hungry.

"Yes, I imagine you are," said Granny Jean. "I have sandwiches in the kitchen." My daughter followed her grandmother, and Bryan and I trailed after her.

While we were eating, I asked Mom about plans for the next day.

"Which church do you think we should attend?"

"The St. Anne folks would like to see the babies," she replied. "Will you be able to go to there?"

My dad had a two-point parish, and taking the four children to that church meant a half-hour drive. I was comfortable driving in familiar places, but not the country roads between the two towns. Bryan would have to come.

"Sounds good to me," I said. "What about you?" I turned to look at Bryan. "Would you drive us?"

"I guess I could, at great personal sacrifice," he said, but he was grinning. He was trying to sound put-upon, but I knew he would be glad to be there, introducing the babies at the neighbouring church.

When Meggie finished her sandwich, she wanted to go tramping in the back yard snow with Daddy. Bryan agreed, and the two of them donned coats, hats and boots.

After they'd left, I showed my parents our photographs, including ones of Geoffrey in the hospital. My mother scrutinized them, looking for similarities among the four of them, and trying to discern family resemblances.

"They're not identical," she said, "but you can certainly tell they're brothers."

Everything is a Big Production

"Yes, but I still mistake them at times." I hated to admit it, since they were my children, and I should have been able to tell them apart.

"How are you managing without your overnight help? Do you think you'd like someone else?" my mother asked. "Because Uncle Louis' niece, Petra, said she'd be willing to help you." Uncle Louis was my Dad's brother-in-law.

"That would be great. The doctor thinks Geoffrey may be ready to come home soon. I can barely manage three babies. I'm sure I'll never cope with four."

"Okay, I'll tell her you're interested."

Bryan drove to a nearby Power Station on Monday, to spend the day working. Driving back, he heard the news about the Challenger space shuttle blowing up.

When he told us, I was horrified at the loss of life, and was particularly touched by the reports of the little girl who had not wanted her mother, a civilian teacher, to go. Thoughts of my own daughter, and our recent separation, made the little girl's loss seem more real to me. It was unusual for me to react like that, though.

On Tuesday, Bryan and I wanted to leave early, to beat the traffic. We didn't achieve our goal, and had to spend a tense half-hour stuck in a traffic jam. Finally, we were able to pull into a restaurant and service our crew. After doing so, the remainder of the trip home was almost pleasant.

Petra, my uncle's niece, arrived at the end of February. A week later, Geoffrey came home from the hospital. With his arrival, my schedule disintegrated. One casualty was the diaper arrangement.

I had been using a diaper service, in an effort to save the environment. Since we didn't have a bathroom on the main floor, we had to carry the dirty diapers upstairs to rinse them. We stored the large, smelly pail of used diapers in the closet off the kitchen, to keep it away from the cats and our inquisitive three-year-old. It required extra effort, but I persevered, and the volunteers followed my lead.

Using cloth diapers, despite the increased work, appealed to the ecologically aware aspect of my personality. However, I did notice that the diapers often leaked which resulted in more laundry, which was also harmful to the environment. So maybe going back to using cloth diapers instead of disposables was not the answer.

I cared about what happened to the environment, I really did. But on top of everything else in my life, it was hard to maintain that focus. Using a diaper service certainly reduced the garbage going to the landfill, but it added to my stress level.

"Mom," I said in a phone conversation, later that week. "It's so much extra work using the diaper service, and I hate using pins. I always jab myself. But I feel guilty about using disposable diapers because they're bad for the environment."

"Listen, Val," my mother admonished me. "I know you care about the environment. You've been recycling religiously the whole time you've been living on your own. But God will forgive you if you're lax in that department for a few months while you get over the most time-consuming part of raising quadruplets."

I tried to take my mother's advice not to feel guilty as I switched to using disposables completely. The issue of disposable diapers would resurface in a few years, and I would find myself in the news again.

Having four babies at home also disrupted the feeding regimen. Just one extra mouth to feed, but it taxed my time management skills. Adding to the hullabaloo was the fact that the boys had started eating solids. Not only did it take longer to feed each baby, but clean up was more time-consuming as well.

We had intended to go to Bala the weekend after Geoffrey had come home from the hospital, in March, as an introductory visit to my grandmother, aunt and uncle. Our plan, as before, was to rise early, and be on the road at 5:00 a.m. We would have arrived in Bala at 7:30 a.m., just in time for the breakfast feeding. However, at 12:30 a.m., I awoke to hear Geoffrey wheezing. He was having trouble catching his breath.

I phoned the doctor, and drove my son to the hospital. He was kept under a humidifier hood, but didn't have to be given extra oxygen. Geoffrey's second homecoming a couple of days later, was permanent, and although we hadn't made it to Bala that time, after that, we were able to make one or two trips a year to visit with my grandmother, before her death in 1991.

In January, my parents, the priest at my church, and I had started thinking about having the boys baptized since we knew Geoffrey would be ready to leave the hospital in a few months. Bryan only wanted to be involved peripherally.

"What's the big deal?" he asked. "We're just going to stuff the babies in the car, go to the church service, baptize them and come home, aren't we?"

Ha! This indicated how much our life had changed. Nothing was simple anymore. Suddenly, everything was a big production.

We started telling our relatives and a few friends that we were having the boys baptized, and we were pleasantly surprised to discover some of them wanted to attend.

Bryan's brother and his wife, from Winnipeg, planned to come since we had asked them to be Alan's godparents. Then Bryan's dad and stepmother decided they would come from Saskatoon, and his aunts from Winnipeg wanted to come as well.

The ceremony was planned for a regular Sunday service in April. The priest at my church invited my father to take part in the service, preaching the sermon and performing the actual baptism.

During the next three months, while doing our regular activities, we anticipated having our families come to visit. I arranged motel accommodations for our out-of-province visitors, and my husband organized a car rental for his dad.

Bryan's dad and stepmother arrived in town the Tuesday prior to the event. Petra and I stayed home while Bryan and Meggie drove to meet them in the rented car. When they arrived home, I could see that Gerry looked much better for having quit smoking and drinking since his last visit. After a half hour introduction to the babies, they were ready to escape to their motel.

My parents arrived on Friday, just after noon, and checked into a motel. An hour later, they came to the house. Since our visitors from Winnipeg were due to arrive at the airport that evening, Bryan and I drove into Toronto to meet them, leaving Petra and my parents to look after Meggie and the babies.

When we arrived home, Bryan's aunt wanted to light up, but we informed her that the rule established by Bryan's dad remained in effect. His aunt could not believe it.

"You mean you'd make your dear old Aunt Betty stand on the porch to smoke a cigarette?" she asked incredulously.

"Yes, I would," said Bryan. "Dad went outside when he smoked, so now it's a house rule." To soften his words, however, he stood outside with her. Later, after his aunts had a cup of tea and a quick peek at the babies, Bryan drove them to their motel.

The next morning, Bryan's aunts and my parents arrived to help feed the babies. Our sons were used to many different people holding them. They didn't make strange, but Petra was at hand if a problem arose. Bryan and I left. The grandparents and great-aunts could enjoy the infant milieu of our house without us.

We picked up two large cakes, with two boys' names on each, and delivered them to the parish hall. Members of the churchwomen's group were decorating the hall, getting ready for the reception after the service. By this time, Bryan realized that we were in for more than just "stuffing the kids in the car, taking them to the church and returning home."

When we got back to the house, Bryan made tea and coffee. My mother had made sandwiches. We ate in shifts, some in the dining room while others stayed with the babies in the family room.

"Mom, I don't have anything to wear," I said, wistfully. "I had to borrow a dress to go to the shower at the hospital last fall. None of my clothes fit me, other than sweatpants and tops."

"Do you have an Eaton's store here? I could select a few outfits and bring them back for you to try on." My mother knew that I didn't like shopping for clothes. Standing and looking at racks of clothing tired me. Having to change in the confined space of a dressing room, often without a chair, was difficult.

Mom also knew that I liked to wear clothes that were easy to get into, such as pull-on tops, and pants with elastic waistbands. Fiddling with buttons, especially small ones frustrated me.

"This is a dressier occasion, Val. I'll try to find a skirt that has only one button. You should be able to manage that."

"Yes, I probably could. Maybe you'll find something I like. Thanks, Mom."

It took four trips, but we finally decided on a pink tweed skirt and jacket, and a matching blouse.

"You won't have to button and unbutton the blouse each time, just undo the top two buttons, and put it on as you would a sweater," my mother said, as she showed me what she'd bought.

"It'll be good to have one decent outfit," I admitted.

Sunday morning was a mad scramble. Meggie planned to wear a pink jacket and matching hat that my mother had made. However, she needed help getting into her dress first. Bryan was ready to go, dressed in a suit with tie, when we met in the hall, going in opposite directions.

"You look good, all gussied up," I complimented him. He didn't even wear a tie to work.

"Thanks," he responded before bustling off to help our daughter. "I'm coming, Meggie, I'll get your dress off the hanger."

Figure 17: Paul, Alan, Geoffrey, Richard

Everything is a Big Production

I entered the bedroom to put my suit on, before going downstairs to help dress the boys in their white Christening gowns with matching bonnets and bootees, all crocheted by my aunt and her friend.

We were five minutes late getting to the church. Our party, four adults carrying four babies and the support staff, followed the choir down the aisle to get to our seats in the front row. Later, when it was time for the baptism, there was a bit more confusion, getting each baby with his godparents. The congregation, many of whom were our volunteers, understood, and waited patiently.

At the reception, after the service, one of our friends used our video camera to record the festivities. The boys sat in their car seats, at one end of the hall. After an hour of socializing and admiring the babies, people started to leave, and we began our own preparations to depart. Feeding time was approaching.

The celebration continued at our house, for family and close friends. Fortunately, there were relatives to act as host–I was too tired.

One friend asked Bryan what had happened to the Jag, which was no longer parked in our backyard.

"It's gone." Bryan sighed. "I sold it to a friend. I knew I wasn't going to have the time, money or energy to work on it any more. Also, we need the money to put new windows in the house this fall."

"You'd had that car for many years," said Bryan's brother. "It must have been sad to see it go."

"It was, but I have the house to work on now."

Our guests made one last tour of the cribs to see the babies. I was sitting in a chair and waved good-bye. Bryan stood at the door to bid our guests farewell.

And Babies Make Seven

With the conclusion of the festivities, and the exodus of our friends and relatives over the next few days, we were back to our everyday lives. Petra was there to help, as were the volunteers. Meggie and I made our weekday trek to nursery school. The visits to the hospital weren't necessary.

But with all four of the babies at home, what was necessary was a new schedule. Sitting at the dining room table, I wrote a timetable with an activity slotted into each hour of the day. I taped it to a kitchen cupboard, visible but unread. In a rare, free moment, I looked at it. No wonder I didn't read it. The writing was too small. Make another!

A perfect timetable would produce a perfectly ordered household. Feeding babies, playing with babies, diapering babies, reading to Meggie, doing the laundry, making a meal...stick to the timetable! It didn't happen.

I despaired of ever finding the perfect timetable. AARGH!

"It doesn't matter, Val," Bryan consoled me. "You're a good mother. The schedule doesn't matter."

My saviour!

13: A Lovely Day in June

Two months later, the Christening was a distant memory. I hadn't written the perfect timetable, but it was irrelevant. Bryan thought I was a good mother, and that was my talisman.

My day still began at 6 a.m. After making a quick trip to the bathroom, and dressing in shorts and a T-shirt, I headed to the boys' bedroom. Geoffrey and Paul were babbling in their cribs.

"Hi guys," I sang softly, not wanting to wake the other two, but their eyes were already open.

Picking Geoffrey up, I cuddled him before taking him to the change table. He seemed to be bigger and heavier than his brothers were, although he wore the same size clothing as Richard. After replacing his diaper and sleeper, I carried him down the back stairs to the family room.

I was happy to have him at home. Not only did it end my daily visits to the hospital, but it also meant my four sons could get to know each other. In addition, Geoffrey would realize that *I* was his mother.

Laying him on his stomach on the floor, I put a rattle and a teething ring within reach before setting the baby gate in the doorway and heading up the stairs to get another baby. I met Petra in the hall carrying Alan and Paul, one in each arm.

"Good morning Petra. Geoffrey's in the family room."

"Morning. I'll take these two down and change them."

We were like the proverbial ships passing in the night. By the time I'd formulated a response, I was at the bedroom door, and she was halfway down the back stairs. Words were superfluous.

"Hi Richard. How are you today?" I picked him up and nuzzled him, taking in his sleepy baby scent. After I changed him, he gave me one of his bright smiles, and made 'Gully, gully, gully' sounds. I carried him down the stairs, holding him in one arm and running my hand along the banister. I handed him over the baby gate to Petra, and she strapped him into his baby seat.

I stayed in the kitchen to prepare breakfast. While mixing a bowl of pablum I could hear, mingled in with the baby noises from the family room, Meggie telling Bryan a story as they walked down the stairs. "...a family of stones and the babies didn't want to jump, so the mummy had to say jump little stone..."

Bryan had helped Meggie dress, and they ate breakfast together, at the dining room table. Meanwhile, I handed the bowl to Petra, who was sitting on the floor with the four baby seats arranged in a half circle around her. She began feeding them while I prepared four bottles of milk. I had made a pot of tea, and I grabbed a cup while I could.

By the time Bryan left for work, Petra had almost finished giving the boys their pablum. I had the bottles ready. She and I sat on the couch with the babies in their seats sitting on the floor facing us. We propped their bottles of milk on a receiving blanket. My daughter wandered in.

"Her TV show must have ended," I thought, glancing at the clock. Sure enough, it was 9:00 a.m.

As each baby finished his bottle, one of us burped him and laid him on the floor. I heard a soft knock on the back door, followed by the door being opened.

"Hi," I called out. "We're in the family room."

It was the physiotherapists from the Infant Stimulation Program, coming for their twice-weekly visits with my sons. They had been coming for six months.

"I can hear the babies," said one, as the two women walked through the kitchen.

They stepped over the baby gate. The babies had been babbling, but they quieted to look at the new arrivals.

One therapist, Fran, took Geoffrey to one side of the room, and the other took Paul to the opposite side. They opened suitcase-type bags and took out rattles, plastic rings and other toys.

Fran sat on the floor with her knees bent. She placed Geoffrey on the floor with his back to her and his legs outstretched. Holding him at the pelvic area, she tipped him back onto his right hip, and then onto his left. After doing that a couple of times, she encouraged him to pick up two cubes, one in each hand, and to bang them together. His shrieks and laughter indicated he enjoyed the interaction. The other therapist was doing similar things with Paul.

The focus of the program was to look for delays in development. In our case, the boys were premature and so any delays might relate to biological factors. They were also making sure there was no onset of cerebral palsy or other conditions.

I stood in the doorway watching them and noticed Alan, pulling himself along the floor with his arms.

"Look, Alan's commando crawling!"

He was squawking as he inched towards the change table. He took a pair of folded socks, stored in the drawer at floor level, and stuck them in his mouth as he rolled over on his back. He gummed them a bit, and then rolled over onto his stomach, reaching to replace them in the drawer.

Meggie walked over to him and sat beside him.

"Good stretching, Alan," Fran said, nodding in approval of his actions.

"Yes, good stretching," my daughter echoed as she thumped him on the back.

"Careful. Be gentle!" I cautioned.

Fran handed her a rattle, saying, "Encourage him to reach for this."

With that situation defused, I relaxed and watched the other therapist putting Paul into a crawling position. I remembered how fifteen years earlier, as I was taking physiotherapy, I'd had to practice crawling before learning to walk.

It had required a lot of thought. I had to stop and think before putting the opposite arm and leg forward at the same time. Paul seemed unconcerned with the mechanics—he just rocked gently on his hands and knees. In another month he'd start moving without any thought to what he was doing.

"Now, in your 'spare time'," Fran said, "you and Bryan can do these exercises with the boys. You can practice at the group meeting, too."

I could hear the quotation marks around the term "spare time" as she spoke, and I rolled my eyes. The group meetings had occurred the second Wednesday of the month. In the morning, I'd phoned the health unit.

"Hi, Fran. It's Val. I'm leaving now."

"OK. I'll round up some helpers and meet you at the front door."

Petra stayed home to look after Meggie. I was on my own, as I loaded my sons into the van.

Driving into the parking lot, I saw Fran and one, or two (after Geoffrey came home) women standing inside the door. They came to meet me as I parked. Each of us took one baby in a car seat into the room where the other babies and moms, participants in the program, were gathered.

Figure 18: Fran and the boys

The other mothers and I played "Pat-a-cake" and "Peek-a-boo" with our babies. I took turns playing with my sons. The therapists were there to help. We exercised the babies by having them reach for a toy, or we encouraged eye movement by waving a toy in front of them. After the morning playtime, two or three helpers assisted getting the babies into the van for the return trip.

The home visit by the therapists lasted an hour and continued until the boys were a year old. After the visit in June, Petra and I checked the boys for wet diapers. Some days we only changed two!

Petra carried two babies upstairs, and I followed with the other two. I could carry a baby in each arm since I no longer needed to hold a railing while ascending stairs.

The previous month, we'd moved the other two cribs upstairs. The four of them were in two rows of two. A large wooden shelving unit against one wall held bags of diapers, blankets and sleepers. Along an adjacent wall was a change table. The room was crowded, but manageable.

Once all four boys had settled in their cribs, three looking ready to sleep and Paul babbling softly, I went downstairs. As I entered the kitchen, I heard Meggie singing softly. She was sitting at the table, playing with a large lump of pink dough.

"I see Petra got the playdough out," I said.

"Yes, that's a turtle." She pointed to one lump of the pink mixture wrapped inside another.

"And this is its blanket." Pulling another lump of dough from what remained, she began rolling it. She was happy playing by herself, which was fortunate. I didn't like having to use the TV as a babysitter, but at times it was the only way I could manage.

Petra had tidied the kitchen while I was with the therapists. I truly appreciated having her there. She was able to look after Meggie, and she could help with the boys whenever I couldn't manage. I *was* finding it easier, though.

I no longer needed to rest while the boys slept, and I tried to get a few chores done. A woman came to vacuum the house once a week, courtesy of my grandmother. The lighter chores: tidying toys and doing the laundry were my responsibility. Bryan helped with kitchen duties when he could.

When the boys woke up, I ferried them downstairs while Petra helped Meggie put the 'turtle' and its 'blanket' in the empty margarine container, its 'home'. With the table cleared, we were able to do lunch.

After the boys had eaten, we propped four bottles of milk on baby blankets as they sat in their baby seats. Petra and I finished our sandwiches. The boys were sitting close enough to touch one another's hands as they flailed their arms.

"Paul, are you holding Alan's hand?" Paul turned to me at the sound of his name, and smiled. Alan turned in my direction, but wasn't as quick to smile.

"Alan, smile at Mummy," ordered Meg as she got down from her chair and patted him on the cheek.

Alan looked at his sister and finally smiled. He looked away again and started banging the block he held in his other hand on the tray of the baby seat. He'd knocked the blankets off when he'd finished his bottle. Paul had finished his bottle too and they both yawned.

"It looks like someone, or maybe even two someones, are ready for bed." I unbuckled Paul, burped him and put him back in his chair. I repeated the procedure with Alan. Petra helped me get one boy in each arm and I headed up the stairs. Petra burped Richard and Geoffrey, and followed me.

When I returned to the kitchen, I called to Meggie. "We have to leave soon to walk to nursery school."

"I don't want to go today," she whined.

"Uh-oh," I thought. "It's going to be one of those days."

"Sure you do," I said with forced gaiety. "It'll be fun. You'll see all your friends, and you can play with the toys, and..."

"I want to stay here with the babies, and you and Petra," she interrupted me.

"Let's go upstairs to clean your hands and do your teeth." My daughter liked going to nursery school, and I didn't sense her heart was really in this rebellion. It was just a matter of form...I hoped.

She raced up the back stairs and I followed her. While she brushed her teeth, I retrieved a sweater from her bedroom. We had fifteen minutes before school started. We were still on track!

When we arrived at the nursery school, my daughter spotted a friend immediately, and she barely noticed my departure. I walked home slowly, enjoying the chance to be outdoors. Flowers were starting to grow in neighbouring gardens...not ours. Trees were budding. Ah, yes! The fresh scents of early summer, a pleasing change to the baby smells pervading our home.

The next year Meggie would go to Senior Kindergarten. A bus would pick her up. Bryan and I could have sent her to Junior Kindergarten instead of sending her to nursery school for another year, but with all the changes at home, we felt it was better keeping her school situation the same.

When I arrived home, Petra had just finished tidying the kitchen.

"We've been given two more bags of clothing." I said. "Do you mind helping me sort through them?"

I knew Petra would help. She was very agreeable, and did whatever I asked, smiling all the while.

We sat in the living room, at the front of the house, and I opened the first bag. I gave half the contents to Petra. "As you look at each item, put the ones that need mending on the table and I'll send them to Mom."

My mother liked to sew. She didn't live close enough to help on a daily basis, but stitching seams or replacing missing buttons was something she *could* do.

"Okay," said Petra. "Do you want to keep pink sleepers? Or not, since they're all boys?"

"If they're the right size and they look clean, keep them. We can't afford to be choosey. I'll have to find another closet to keep these in, though."

Our house had neither a basement nor attic suitable for storage. Bryan had built a large cupboard over the front stairs to hold additional clothing, sheets and blankets. Even with that though, green garbage bags filled with garments were often stuck under tables or in corners. We had just finished putting the clothes into piles, and I was stuffing the ones that needed mending back into the bag, when we heard lusty cries up the front stairs.

We looked at each other. It was show time! Four babies crying truly was the Halleluiah Chorus, as my father-in-law called it. As I went up the stairs, and the sound intensified, I reminded myself that human nature being what it is; I would soon forget this part of the ordeal.

Nevertheless, it did help to keep a sense of humour. In that much din it was hard to carry on a conversation, so those of us who weren't hollering often laughed. When Meggie was there, she joined in; looking from my face to Bryan's to Petra's, as if trying to figure out the joke.

Petra followed me up the stairs and into the bedroom. She took Alan and Paul downstairs, one in each arm. I followed her with Geoff, and placed him on the floor in the family room. She started changing Paul while I went to get Richard. The bawling abated as each baby received the necessary attention.

It was a warm, sunny day, and I suggested we take the babies for a walk around the block. As I dressed the boys for an outside jaunt, Petra retrieved the two used twin strollers that we stored on the back porch. We had bought them after selling the four single strollers we had been given in August.

Figure 19: L to R: Geoffrey, Richard (back), Paul, Alan (front)

Petra put Alan and Geoff facing each other in one, and I put Richard facing Paul in the other. As we walked along the street, Richard and Paul kicked at each other. Soon their bootees had fallen off, and I stopped.

A Lovely Day in June

"Ba ba ba," I said in imitation of Paul, who was trying to reach across to Richard, who was howling and kicking. I replaced the foot coverings.

"Okay, guys, we're going. Sh-sh-sh."

I started pushing the stroller again, jiggling it to soothe them. Petra began moving as soon as she saw we were underway, trying to calm Geoffrey and Alan. As we walked, we passed the house where the president of the twin's club lived.

After our initial visit the summer before, Bryan and I had started attending the monthly meetings in November. Because of our involvement, the club changed its name from a twins group to the Peterborough and Area Multiple Births Association.

Listening to speakers and talking with other parents of multiples wasn't the only aspect of the club I enjoyed. Twice a year they held clothing sales at the local farmer's market and I attended as both a buyer and a seller.

After our walk, Petra took the boys into the family room and fed them a bowl of cereal. I drove to get Meggie from nursery school, stopping in to pick up a bag of milk on the way home.

As I walked in the back door, I heard Petra in the family room, saying, "Open your mouth Alan."

I smiled to myself, thinking, "Alan must be disrupting the tempo."

Using one bowl and one spoon, there was a rhythm to feeding the four boys. Dip into the food, shovel into a mouth; dip into the food, shovel into a mouth. After two more dips and shovels, the first was waiting for more food. And so it went, until the food was gone.

144

And Babies Make Seven

Although the boys had been eating solids for four months, it was still messy. Splotches of pablum adorned hands and faces; blobs of gray goo stuck to sleepers and seats.

Meggie had stationed herself in the living room and was watching TV. With things under control for the moment, I started preparing dinner. A half hour later, I took a break from food preparation to help Petra clean hands and faces and remove the babies from their seats. After ensuring the baby gate was secure, Petra went upstairs.

Bryan arrived home shortly thereafter. As the boys learned to crawl, one, two, three or four boys crawled to the gate, sat down, and cried or gurgled when they heard Bryan entering the house. Our daughter ran in from the living room.

It was easy to ascertain Bryan's mood: if it had been a good day, he escaped up the back stairs to change, saying a quick "Hi Val" as he passed. Returning in his jeans and T-shirt, he laid on his back in the family room with the boys crawling over him, squealing in delight.

On the other hand, a tiring day meant he ran up the back stairs and stayed in our bedroom reading. On those days, Bryan was compelled to join the maelstrom after I called to say dinner was ready.

"Put Paul in the swing-o-matic. Geoffrey, Alan and Richard can go in the baby seats.

"Or does anyone look tired?" I inquired optimistically.

Petra came down the stairs and looked in the family room. "Richard might go down for a while. Do you want me to see if he will?"

"Yes, please," I said, getting four plates out of the cupboard. Bryan carried Paul to the dining room. While Petra was upstairs with Richard, Bryan got Meggie and the other babies settled in the dining room. After

145

having set the table, I carried the food in. Petra returned, and we sat at the dining room table. Immediately we heard Richard crying.

"You get him, I'll get the baby seat," I said to Petra as we both stood.

With the three babies close enough that Bryan, Petra or I could jiggle them with a foot if needed, and Paul happily amused in the swing, we finished dinner. Afterwards Bryan took care of Meggie, watching TV until bath time.

Petra gave Alan and Paul their bottles while I did the same with Geoffrey and Richard. After we finished, Petra and I took the babies upstairs, changed them and put them to bed.

After that, I waited downstairs until Bryan had finished his bedtime routine with Meggie. When he came downstairs, I went upstairs to kiss her good night before she fell asleep.

Bryan and I shared a pot of tea in the living room after quietness had descended.

"Did Meggie want you to read Heidi again?" I asked him.

"Yes, I finished it last night, and I thought she'd want another book, but no, she wants me to read it again."

"How many times is this?"

"The fourth, I think. I've lost track. I've nearly had my fill of grandfathers, mountains and goats!" Bryan smiled as he said it, indicating he didn't really mind.

We finished our tea. It was 9:30, and Petra was in her bedroom. It was time for us to retire as well.

We carried our dishes into the kitchen, turning off lights as we went. I checked the back door and ascended the back stairs while Bryan checked the front door, and went up the front stairs. We met in the hallway and looked in on our daughter. She was sleeping peacefully, lying crossways in the bed. Bryan entered her bedroom to straighten her, and I went to the other end of the hall to check the boys. They were asleep. Bryan and I went into our bedroom.

As I fell asleep, I counted my blessings. The babies slept through most nights, and all my kids were healthy. My good mother status had expanded to include being a busy mother as well. I was busier than I wanted to be, perhaps, but for so many years, my activity had been restricted. This felt good.

14: One Four-Year-Old and Four One-Year-Olds

One July day, I woke up remembering a morning in 1976, when I had finished university, but hadn't found work. I had lain in bed, panic-stricken, because I had nothing to do.

Ten years later, I wasn't likely to suffer a panic attack envisioning a task-free day. Being a mother to five children meant there was always much to do. It was a given that all the babies had to be fed, but some days one drank his bottle and was happy. Other days another drank his bottle and was happy. The chance that all four babies would drink their bottles and be happy at the same time was infinitesimally small!

It was not just feeding times that created an ambience of chaos. Richard could have diaper rash. Alan could have an earache. Geoffrey or Paul might have an asthma attack, necessitating a quick phone call to the doctor, or a trip to his office. Once again, my present situation seemed to be a replay of a past life.

In 1978, living with my grandparents, I had been busy, but I hadn't accomplished a lot. Those feelings resurfaced in the mid 1980s. So much to do...so little to show for it...

It was a Saturday, and Bryan was home. I heard cries from the bedroom next door. My time for reflection had ended. It was 3:00 p.m. before I had another chance to stop and think.

The boys were in the family room, playing, and Meggie was in the living room watching TV. It was unexpectedly quiet as Bryan and I

148

shared a pot of tea, sitting at the kitchen table. We were discussing the boys' first birthday party, to take place in a month.

"I think we should have an adult party. We don't want to have a group of one-year-old babies here, do we?" I asked

"Good Lord, no!" He sounded horrified at the mere mention of such a possibility. "But who would we invite?"

"We could invite the volunteers who helped us for the past year but who aren't coming anymore. They might enjoy seeing the boys. We still have a bit of time…"

I stopped talking as Alan and Richard crawled into the kitchen. They were both crying. Richard came to me and I scooped him up. Alan went to Bryan, who picked him up and plunked him on his knee, which stopped the crying.

"How's my Alan today?" he asked. Geoffrey and Paul had followed the others into the kitchen, and their cries echoed those of Richard. Bryan and I looked at each other and started laughing. I stood and patted Richard on the back.

Petra was upstairs and hearing the cacophony, she came down to offer assistance.

"Yes, it must be time to change diapers," I agreed.

A half hour later, when everybody was happy again, Petra came into the living room where Bryan and I had migrated.

"I've decided to go to hairdressing school," she said. "I'll have to leave next month."

"We knew you wouldn't stay forever, Petra," I said. "But, we'll miss you."

"I can't imagine anyone staying here if they didn't have to," Bryan said, and he laughed.

One Four-Year-Old and Four One-Year-Olds

"That's not true," said Petra. "I've really enjoyed living with you and helping to look after Meggie and the boys. I'm going to miss you all."

"Well, at least you'll be here for the boys' party," I said.

"Yes. I'm looking forward to that," she said. Hearing a wail from upstairs she added, "I'll go and see what Meggie wants."

Turning to Bryan I said, "I'll be sad to see Petra leave, but maybe we've reached the point where we can manage without live-in help. What do you think?"

"It's up to you, Val. You're the one who's alone with the kids all day. I have to go to work. Do *you* think you'll be able to manage?"

"It's certainly easier with Petra here, but, if she wasn't here…" I paused, lost in thought. The boys weren't as demanding. They could wait for a diaper change, if need be. They sat in baby seats to eat, which allowed me to prop bottles. I'd had six months to get used to having five children.

Bryan waited, watching me expectantly. "Well?"

"Yes, I can do it," I said. I almost added, "I think…" belying my words, but I stopped myself.

Meggie ran into the room and turned the TV on. Bryan and I retreated to the kitchen.

"Did you stop for donuts again after Meggie's gym lesson?"

She took gymnastics or "gym-antics" as she called them, each Saturday morning. It gave her a chance to learn to somersault, and to walk backwards along a small, raised platform. She wore a pink gym suit, which looked good with her fair hair and rosy cheeks.

"Yes, we did," he said. "This is the only time I get to spend alone with her, and I want her to have memories that'll last a lifetime."

"Yes, I know. I think it's important for the two of you to have time together." I paused, and then added, "I almost forgot to tell you; the photographer from the paper called while you were out. He's offered to take a picture of the boys, and he'll only charge for the cost of processing."

"That's great! As a professional, I can imagine he must charge a lot. Did he say where he wants to take the picture?"

"The lighting's better outside. He suggested going to Jackson Park. It's in the city, and the trees will provide shade."

"That makes sense, and the park will be a good backdrop. Will you phone him next week to set it up?" Bryan asked. "We can do it next Saturday."

"Yes, I'll do that."

Figure 20: First birthday party

Dinner was a haphazard affair, with Meggie and Bryan sitting at the table to eat, while Petra and I juggled babies and bottles and tried to grab food for ourselves as well. "Will I be able to manage after she leaves?" I wondered. "Yes, Bryan and I will figure something out. The

151

guys are almost old enough to sit in highchairs and eat with us…I can hardly wait!"

We held the boys' party the last Saturday in August. On a warm and sunny afternoon, we set out the wading pool, filled with a couple inches of water. The boys sat in it or crawled around on their hands and knees. Meggie joined them, splashing and causing shrieks and squeals in response.

Six women, four volunteers from the church and a couple of women from the sorority group of babysitters, came to watch the children as they played in the pool. We had tea and cookies, and reminisced about events of the last year.

I asked the woman who had been my volunteer coordinator how she'd felt when my mother had phoned in a panic because she was alone.

"Oh, yes," she said, remembering. "Your poor mother."

"Bryan and I had gone away overnight before Geoffrey came home," I explained to the others, "and Mom had agreed to come and babysit. I promised she wouldn't be here on her own during the day, but then one volunteer had to leave before another arrived."

"She managed, though." The volunteer coordinator finished the story. "We talked, and the volunteer arrived a short time later."

By three o'clock, people were getting ready to leave, and the kids wanted to dry off and move indoors. After a quick supper and bedtime routine, the kids were ready to go to bed.

My parents arrived the next day, laden with gifts. Meggie was in charge of handing them out, after I read the names to her. She helped each boy unwrap his present, and then gave it to him.

"Look, Alan, it's a telephone"

"Here Geoffrey, it's some blocks"

"Paul, some more blocks—look!"

"Oh look, Richard…what's this Mum?"

I leaned forward. "It's a shape sorter. You shake all the pieces out and then you have to put them back. Each piece fits through one hole."

"And here's a present for Meggie," I handed her one with her name on it.

"Ohhhhh," she said, laughing with delight. She ripped the paper off and took it to her grandmother. Granny Jean wanted to show her how to use the cork and knitting spool. She could make long strings of knitted wool and with Granny's help form it into a potholder.

"Thanks, Mom and Dad," I said. "This is great."

Later in the day, there was a knock on the front door. We knew what to expect, although the kids didn't. Our friends had arrived a half hour earlier to tell us what they'd planned. They wanted to celebrate their goddaughter's first anniversary of becoming a big sister.

I answered the door, and ushered the giant white rabbit, holding a bouquet of balloons, into the living room.

Bryan called the kids, "Meggie, Geoffrey, Alan, Richard, Paul, come and see who's here!"

Five kids ran into the living room, pushing, shoving and tripping over each other to be first. My friend Dawn helped Meggie to sit on the couch, and Bryan and I sat the babies beside her. Two were crying, and the other two were sucking their thumbs. Meggie's eyes almost popped out of her head.

The rabbit sang "Happy Anniversary to You" and presented the bouquet of balloons to Meggie, who was stunned into silence—quite a feat!

We urged the rabbit to sit on the couch while we took a picture. After that, Dawn and I thanked the rabbit several times. I hoped it wasn't her first job, or it might well have been her last!

Figure 21: The Giant Rabbit

Shortly after she left, our friends took their leave too. We said our good-byes amid screams and shouts. Geoffrey and Paul were each trying to get on the same riding toy.

Bryan picked up Geoffrey and a baby book that was lying close by, leaving Paul to ride the toy. My parents helped Bryan amuse the children in the family room. With tranquility restored for the moment, I made final preparations for dinner.

My parents had to leave the next day. It had been a quick visit, but short doses of our family were as much as they could take. Petra moved out a few days later. The summer was over and Meggie started senior kindergarten. I found it strange at first, being the only adult in the house for a good part of the day.

Reading the paper one evening, I saw an ad for a parenting course being offered at the health unit. The Systematic Training for Effective Parenting (STEP) program advised allowing natural or logical consequences to follow from the child's actions, making punishment unnecessary. This was just what I needed!

At the first meeting, Bryan delighted in telling the other participants that we had one four-year-old and four one-year-olds. We were given a workbook of responses and actions when confronted with disciplinary problems. I cut the pages out and taped them to the kitchen cupboards so I could read and absorb the information, while doing dishes and making meals.

One day a friend, who had taken the course with me, came to visit with her four-year-old daughter. I showed her what I'd done with the workbook. Later, I was startled when, as she was getting ready to leave, she rushed down the stairs and into the kitchen saying, "What do I do when the kid says she won't come?"

Laughing, I watched her speed-read through the sections until she came to the one dealing with recalcitrant children. She ran back upstairs to use the proper language with her daughter, to convince her it was time to leave.

A parenting course provided hints about raising children, but the spiritual aspect of my personality needed nurturing too. I had taken my daughter to church when she was a baby, and I wanted to be able to take the boys too. Since it promised him an hour or two alone in the house, Bryan was happy to help get the kids ready. However, I needed assistance when I arrived at the church, as well.

One Four-Year-Old and Four One-Year-Olds

"Hello, is Catharine there?" I was phoning the daughter of the rector of my church, who was fifteen and had been babysitting for us since we'd moved to the house three years previously.

She came to the phone, and I continued, "I'm going to bring the five kids to church tomorrow, for the 10:30 service. Could you and three other girls meet me in the parking lot, to help me carry the boys in?"

"Sure. No problem."

We arranged a meeting time, said good-bye and hung up. With that done, I called the curate who lived in an apartment next to the church.

"I'm planning to drive the five kids to church tomorrow, and I was wondering if you could move your car so I could park next to the door to unload them?"

"Yes, I could do that. Anybody who wants to bring five kids to church deserves a little help."

"You're sure you don't mind?"

"Of course I mind." He paused and laughed. "No, seriously, it's no problem at all. I'll just put my car in the parking lot after the 8:30 service, and my parking spot will be available."

"Thanks. I appreciate this."

Thereafter, I phoned him on Saturday when I was planning to attend church the next day. This arrangement ended the next year, when he transferred to another parish. By then I was able to manage using a regular parking spot on the street.

When I first started attending church with children in tow, however, I relied on the teenage girls to help me carry my sons into the basement of the church. After we left them in the nursery, one of the girls took my daughter to Sunday school in the church hall.

I had grown up attending church and it seemed natural to do the same for my children. My belief in and attitude towards God had changed in my later teens. I felt obliged to go to church to thank God for a second chance at life. I also tried to understand why I had lived and my friends hadn't. Over the years, however, my views changed.

I realized that if I believed God was responsible for me having survived the accident, then I had to believe God was also responsible for my friends not surviving. I could not believe that.

I continued to attend church, even after this revelation. I had to go. The part of me that had glimpsed death felt an inexplicable connection to being in church.

When I met Bryan, I realized that he didn't have the same faith belief I had. We accepted our different beliefs--he didn't try to change me and I didn't try to change him. However, as we discussed our life views, I saw the sense in his.

He believed it was pointless to try to discern a reason for either the tragedy or the miraculous birth. Neither could be changed. Nevertheless, the part of my personality that needed to believe in a power greater than myself, (in this regard I was unlike Bryan) wanted to attend church. On occasion, I was too tired to take part in the service. I simply sat and enjoyed being alone with my thoughts.

Every Sunday that fall, I went to church with the children Bryan and I loaded everyone into the van at home, and teenage girls helped me unload them at the church. Having time alone during the service was worth the hassle.

A few months later, it was December. Geoffrey, Alan, Richard and Paul were one year old and Meggie was four and a half. As we celebrated

One Four-Year-Old and Four One-Year-Olds

Christmas, Bryan and I rejoiced that we had survived our first complete year with five children.

As the children unwrapped presents, I sat on the couch with a pen and pad of paper. As the shredded paper accumulated on the floor, I tried to keep track of who got what from whom, in hopes of sending thank you letters on behalf of my kids.

Over the next several months, I wrote letters to understanding relatives: "Thank you for the gift. I'm not sure what it was…"

15: On My Own

As 1987 began, Petra, our live-in helper, had been gone for four months. My days were hectic, but busy days had meant happy days, when I'd had help. Would that feeling persist?

Being on my own did give me a chance to get to know each boy better. Alan liked to do things for himself, and Paul liked to stay up later at night. Geoffrey was happy-go-lucky. Richard was quiet and easy to please. Although I was beginning to recognize that each boy was an individual, a herd mentality still tended to dominate my thinking.

This was evident when I took my sons to the doctor's for their wellness visits. I preferred taking them together. Each trip required effort, whether I took two babies or four, and taking them all in one trip meant fewer trips. Before Geoffrey had come home, I had taken the three babies together, with two volunteers to help. Adding one more baby to the mix did not require more volunteer help, but it did call for extra concentration from the nurse.

One day in February, I phoned to arrange an eighteen-month wellness visit. Plan ahead was my new motto. I had to schedule it for the next week to get four time slots together.

On the appointed day, I carried Geoffrey from the van to the building and we walked into the office. One of my volunteer helpers followed me in with Alan, and she stayed with the two of them while I helped another volunteer with Paul and Richard. We didn't have to report to the nurse's station. The increased noise level proclaimed our arrival.

On My Own

While my two helpers and I took the boys' snowsuits off and tried to interest them in toys, the nurse got their charts out. I took each tot to her in turn. She weighed him and measured his height.

It was time for an inoculation. This was the time for increased concentration...the nurse had to get four needles ready, and then ensure that each boy got only one injection.

At the invitation of the nurse, I entered the examining room, and sat down opposite the doctor with my son on my lap.

"This is..." the doctor consulted the chart, "Richard. How's his appetite?"

"Um," I said, and paused. It was an annoying habit, but I'd prefaced my speech with that word for years. "Richard's appetite..."   I tried to remember. Was Richard the one who'd eaten everything, or was that Geoffrey? Had Richard refused to eat last night? Or had it been Paul? The doctor looked at me questioningly.

"Richard's appetite..." I started again. "I don't think he's having any problems." I ended lamely.

After the checkup, I returned Richard to the volunteers, and took in a brother.

"What about Alan's bowel movements?" asked the doctor, after consulting his chart. We repeated the process.

"Um, Alan's bowel movements..." I tried to remember, smiling as I looked up and to my right, as if the memory might be locked in that part of my brain. I finally repeated, "I don't think he's having any problems."

And so it went, with questions about Geoffrey and Paul. I tried to remember, I really did, but it was all a blur. I was certain that if there had been any serious problems, I would have remembered. Well, I might've remembered.

Fortunately, the doctor accepted my standard reply, "I don't think there are any problems."

As the doctor tracked each boy's height, weight and head circumference, he was able to make his own deductions, and he was pleased with their progress.

When we finished at the doctor's, I thanked the women who had helped me, and dropped them off as I drove home. Arriving home after spending more than an hour at the doctor's, I was glad to put the babies in the family room, set up the gate, and brew myself a pot of tea. I needed time to recuperate, and I could ignore the squabbling for ten or twenty minutes. Thus fortified, I entered the fray. I detected that someone needed a diaper change.

While changing diapers and afterwards watching my sons play together, I thought about my need to have order and routine in my life. Whether it was because of the brain injury or not, it was the way I was. Nevertheless, letting the boys express their individuality was important. I had done that with my daughter when she was young.

"Of course," I thought, "it's much easier to let your child be a free spirit when she's a singleton."

With four children the same age, I was inclined to treat them as one multi-faceted child. While it wouldn't be detrimental to them at this young age, I knew the time was coming when I would have to recognize that the facets belonged to four separate people.

"Once they start talking," I thought, "it'll be easier to see them as individuals. They'll start to develop their own identities. When that happens, though, the Hallelujah Chorus will grow into the Tower of Babel. How will I handle that?"

On My Own

My daughter liked talking, and already I didn't always listen with rapt attention. If they were all like her, could I process four or five different conversations at once?

As I relaxed in the chair that day in February and listened to my sons, I realized we were in a Catch-22 situation. Because they, and occasionally even Bryan and I, understood what the sounds meant, they didn't feel a need to transform those sounds into words. I did notice, however, that when one of them was making noises, it was broken into phrases and sentences, with inflection.

"He probably thinks he's talking," I mused. And if one of his brothers replied, it was comical...incomprehensible, but comical.

Alan cried in protest, and it jolted me out of my reverie. Richard had grabbed the rattle he'd been trying to reach. I had to get back to work. Ah...the joys of parenthood.

Soon after, my daughter arrived home. She was bubbling over with tales of what had happened at kindergarten. I listened with half an ear as I strapped the boys into high chairs.

Meggie ate her lunch sitting on the couch in the living room, watching Sesame Street on TV. I fed the boys, sitting on a chair in the dining room, with their highchairs arranged in a semi-circle around me. My daughter and I could talk, and the boys added their voices to the noise of the television program.

After lunch, I dropped her at a friend's and took my sons to the library. I had taken Meggie when she was that age because she'd enjoyed story time. Thinking my sons would enjoy it as well, I bundled them in snowsuits and strapped them in the van.

And Babies Make Seven

It proved to be a frustrating experience. I left the library as soon as story hour was over. That evening, I phoned my neighbour to recount my adventure.

"What happened when you arrived?" She asked.

"Things started off well. Richard and Paul were on my lap, sort of, with Alan and Geoffrey beside me. After a few minutes, three of them were interested in the story, but Alan lost interest and wandered off. I couldn't get up to chase him. I didn't want to call him, which would've interrupted the story for the others, so I tried to will him back to me. However, he wasn't tuning in to me—he just strolled around, with his thumb in his mouth. The curtain was pulled, separating the corner we were in from the rest of the library, and luckily he didn't try to go under it. He finally came back to where I was and sat beside me until the story ended."

My neighbour was chuckling by the time I finished. I hadn't been amused at the time, but in retelling the tale, I felt better. We said goodbye and hung up.

After that trip, I decided taking the boys out was not worth the hassle, unless it was necessary, such as to a doctor's appointment. My sons didn't need the extra stimulation. It was easier to stay home.

However, I could not stay home every day. I had to buy food, for instance. Fortunately, one of my friends who had a son the same age as mine, offered to bring him to my house and stay with the five of them while I went grocery shopping. She thought it was fun (there's no accounting for taste!) and it was her way to help.

After I arrived home, my friend helped me carry the groceries into the house.

"Val," she said, "Your groceries are always so heavy."

"Sorry about that," I said, as if it was my fault.

163

On My Own

My friend left shortly after, but she came faithfully every week for several months before other family commitments on her part made it impossible for her to do so.

One reason for the weight of my groceries, perhaps, was that I was still buying baby food in glass jars, but soon the boys would want grownup food. I suggested to Bryan that we buy a freezer so I could buy bread and frozen food on sale.

We bought a chest freezer in April, and put it in the family room, since we couldn't get it into the basement. Although we did need it to store extra food, it also worked well as a change table.

On those spring days in 1987, when I was at home with all five children, we often played ring-around-the-rosy, but if one boy didn't fall down at the proper time, Meggie stomped over and made him. She was perplexed when he started screaming. Did he not know what he was supposed to do?

Other times we would sit in a circle and play "the wheels on the bus." Meggie copied my hand gestures, but the boys didn't. She often put her wheeling hands right in front of her brother's face, encouraging him to copy her actions. It didn't always produce the desired results.

"This is a good age," I thought. "The five of them get along well together."

A couple of months later, Bryan and I were discussing what to do that summer. Since we were still in a harmonious stage, I suggested a driving holiday. Bryan agreed. We had budgetary constraints, but a motor holiday was permissible.

We stopped talking as Richard came into the kitchen on a riding toy with Paul crawling behind. When Richard stopped, Paul grabbed the back of the toy, raised himself to his feet and tried to push his brother off, howling in frustration. Richard screamed in response. I sidestepped the two of them and reached for another riding toy. I gave it to Paul, who calmed down once he had his own toy to ride.

Glad to have peace restored for a minute, I resumed the conversation, "We could do a big circuit, driving to Strathroy, and then up the Bruce Peninsula. We could cross on the ferry to the Manitoulin Island, and then drive home through Sudbury. Our friends in Strathroy invited us to visit them, and we have other friends on the Island we could visit."

"Are we sure we want to visit with people crazy enough to invite all of us to visit...at the same time?"

I laughed. "They aren't crazy–they just can't imagine what it'll be like."

"Okay, let's do it. They won't need imagination, they'll have reality." My husband responded.

I made a couple of phone calls. Afterwards I told Bryan that I had arranged our vacation, but he was having second thoughts.

"It's not a vacation," he grumbled. "It's a change of work location. The work doesn't change; we just do it in a different place."

In July, we went traveling, but I found it much easier with a five-year-old and four nearly two-year-olds. I packed easy-to-eat finger food, such as spoon size shredded wheat and graham crackers. I also took a large thermos of cold water with a training cup for the boys and a plastic cup for Meggie.

I became adept at moving around the van as we travelled, handing out pieces of food, or a cup of water. I did have to sit on the bench to pour the water, though.

Our friends in Strathroy had an above ground pool in their back yard and we introduced the boys to swimming. Meggie had had a couple years of swimming lessons, and she enjoyed the chance to swim with her dad. After the kids went to bed, we adults had the pool to ourselves.

We left Strathroy after a few days, and drove to Tobermory. On the ferry, Bryan walked around holding Meggie by the hand, with the four boys on harnesses, while I sat in the lounge area and tried not to be seasick. He recounted later that many people had stopped him to ask about the children. After a few times his veneer of civility wore off, and he struggled to answer without gritting his teeth.

After landing in South Baymouth, we drove to our friends' house in Manitowaning. They were happy to see us, and were prepared for the invasion. Their two teenage sons, however, chose to stay with friends for the duration. (I didn't blame them!)

I enjoyed being in Manitowaning again, and introducing my family to people who had known me before, as a teenager. One way to erase the image of "the girl who was in the accident" was to arrive with quadruplets, I discovered.

We returned home after our week away, refreshed from the change of job location. Getting away, not only from home, but also from the reason for us being there, would be delightful.

We'd been able to have a weekend off the two previous years, because our daughter had visited with my parents, but it was impossible for them to do it now that we had five children. I wanted, no ... I *needed* a weekend away with my husband, and I was willing to spend time organizing it.

Over the years, I tried many babysitting arrangements to achieve this goal. One year we traded with another couple who also had five children. Each couple had one weekend living with ten children--a seven year old boy, five eight year old boys, a couple of ten year old girls, an eleven year old and twelve year old girl. Our weekend with the crew brought to mind the children's camp I had attended as a youth.

For our holiday in 1987, we hired two sisters, each of whom had babysat Meggie for us, to stay with the five children so we could have one night at a motel in a nearby town.

The next month, August, we celebrated the boys' second birthday by inviting our next-door neighbours over for a party. Five boys, our sons at age two and the neighbour's at two-and-a-half sat together but played individually. Meggie and her little girlfriend played with their dolls. Bryan and I visited with our friends, having tea and cookies, but we knew the time was fast approaching when the boys would realize *they* were the ones who should be enjoying the sweets.

In September, the boys started going to nursery school. I had wondered if we'd be able to afford sending two children to nursery school, and now we were sending four. We were fortunate that the nursery school Meggie had attended not only accepted children in diapers, as the boys were, but was also subsidized.

Since the boys were only two years old, we enrolled each boy for two mornings a week. The pediatrician encouraged us to mix the pairings, rather than always sending the same two together. I kept track of who went on which day by writing their initials on a calendar—GA GR GP AR AP RP. Monday to Thursday mornings, I only had two children at home.

"This must be what it's like to have twins," I thought. "Only having two kids at home is much easier."

I thought I was headed straight towards a life of ease, as the children became ever more involved in school. However, the road curved and I was unprepared not only for it but for the resulting downward spiral as well.

16: Descent into Darkness

As September rolled into October, I felt in control of my life. I thought I was coping. Four mornings a week, I had a reduced workload. Although I no longer had volunteers coming in to help regularly, I did have some respite, some breathing room.

October became November and as the days got shorter so did my temper. The kids were too noisy, I was too tired, and I had trouble making simple decisions. (I phoned my neighbour to ask her what to feed the kids for lunch. "Have you got bread and peanut butter, Val?" she asked me. At my affirmative reply she replied, "Give them peanut butter sandwiches!")

One day, when Bryan came home from work, he found me lying on the couch in the family room. The boys were playing on the floor beside the couch and Meggie was watching TV in the living room. There was nothing ready for dinner. I couldn't even rouse myself to greet him.

I was so far into my own despair that I couldn't see Bryan's point of view was different than mine. While I thought nothing was good and everything was bad, the house was messy and the kids were mischievous, Bryan thought the house was the same as it always had been. When he tried to say our life hadn't really deteriorated, I refused to believe him.

Meanwhile, each new day was a fresh start. I did what I could, getting the boys off to nursery school, and Meggie to kindergarten. But gradually over the day, I wound down, and by late afternoon, I had disconnected again.

And Babies Make Seven

Each day that Bryan came home to find me lying on the couch, he became more concerned because, he told me later, nothing he did could lift me out of my funk. He saw a personality change, and my lack of energy alarmed him.

This scenario occurred once or twice a week, but soon began to happen more frequently. Bryan said later that he had found it increasingly difficult to work an eight-hour day, only to return home, and suddenly discover he was responsible for childcare and meal preparation as well. He was scared because while he could look after the kids and make supper if need be, he could not rescue me from my personal turmoil.

My husband suggested I go to the doctor to have my blood checked. I had been anemic since my teen years so it seemed a reasonable assumption. The next week I made an appointment with my doctor, and had my blood tested. It was fine. She referred me to a counselor.

What a relief to be able to talk to someone! I told the counselor that the noisy confusion of *my* life seemed excessive, and because I could not deal with it, I either yelled at my kids or ignored them. Then I worried they would think I didn't love them. How could my children know it was not *them* I couldn't tolerate, but the noise and confusion that four (and sometimes five) of them created?

While the kids were playing (noisily) or squabbling (noisily) I didn't know what to do. I had written about how I was feeling when I'd gone through traumatic times as a teenager and it seemed natural to do it again. The kids were happy, yelling, screaming, and even laughing, but all I heard was the volume of noise and it distressed me. I sat at the dining room table and put pen to paper.

What right did I have to be angry? I should have been enjoying my children, but I couldn't. I was upset and very angry. I dragged myself to the counseling appointments. After several months, I was referred to a psychiatrist who prescribed anti-depressants.

Through it all, I wrote and with the medication to help, as my anger flowed onto the paper, it left me calmer and better able to deal with the quadraphonic quarreling and TV blaring.

One day, during a lull, I thought, "This is my job, my career, and many people have jobs they dislike at times. Once the children are grown, my job will be finished. I'll be ready to enjoy empty-nest syndrome."

That thought kept me going for a while, but soon I was overwhelmed by feelings of guilt and anger again. Nothing gave me a permanent passage to peace. I wanted to cry, but couldn't. I complained to my husband without realizing that my constant barrage of criticism was having an effect on him as well. My counselor suggested Bryan and I attend a session together.

"As soon as I come in the door after a day's work," he told the counselor, "she pounces on me with a litany of problems. But she complains about things I can't fix. I want to help her, but I can't. It's very frustrating.

"She finds fault with everything--the kids misbehave...the house is messy...she's stuck at home all day. I do what I can, getting the kids to put their toys away, and I tidy the kitchen, but it's never enough. I wish I could stay home to be more help, but I can't. I have to go to my job.

"Val doesn't experience negative emotions the way most people do, and she won't remember that she's depressed right now," he added. "But I will."

I listened to the exchange, but was indifferent to it. We could've been talking about someone else. The counselor and Bryan concluded their talk. The counselor looked at me, inviting a response, but I just shook my head. I was too tired to add anything. Bryan and I left the office and returned home.

At my next visit, the counselor and I expanded our discussion. While talking about my present situation, I explained that I'd received a brain injury seventeen years previously. How did I feel about that? I didn't know. My emotional feedback line was short-circuited.

I did remember that as a teen fighting to regain my life in 1970 I had often thought it might have been easier if I'd died. When I came out of the coma, I was seventeen years old, but functioned as a baby. I relearned how to walk and talk properly and feed myself over many months rather than years, but there were times when I'd wondered if the struggle had been worth it.

By the end of that decade, when I met Bryan and married him, I realized it had been worth it, and I was glad to be alive. However, in the confusion and chaos of the mid 1980s, that feeling resurfaced.

"If I died," I told my counselor, "I wouldn't have to deal with this."

It was true, but saying it did not mean I had ulterior motives of ending my life. It was simply a statement of fact. Talk of self-destruction rang alarm bells for the counselor, though. If I were thinking of suicide, would that put the children at risk? His duty was clear.

When I told Bryan that the counselor had mentioned having the Children's Aid Society (CAS) intervene, he was furious.

"Val, you'd better tone down what you're saying to him. If he's talking of bringing in the CAS, we could lose the kids and we'll never get them back."

Bryan decided to attend a counseling session on his own, to reassure the counselor that I did not always view the glass as being half-empty. He was worried about me, but he also had a deep-seated fear of CAS involvement, I discovered later.

When he told me about the session, (years later when I was ready to hear it) he recalled that they had discussed how being an engineer affected his manner of dealing with my depression. Bryan's training had equipped him to find solutions to problems. Since that was what he did at work, it was what he wanted to do when I griped at him. To come home to a mess for which he had no solution was a personal insult.

"Val doesn't expect you to solve her problems," the counselor had told him, "*all* she wants you to do is listen to her tale of woe."

Bryan was dumbfounded. That was all? No calculations, formulae or measurements?

The counselor reassured him, "*You* don't have to solve the confusion of her life, just listen as she tells you about it. But don't worry; many engineers think the way you do."

The week before my next appointment, I didn't know Bryan had received this earth-shattering revelation. What I did know was that when I told Bryan what was happening, he was less upset. That week my writing wasn't as vitriolic.

At my next session, the counselor gave me a task. I had to tell each child I loved him or her twice a day. Every day I told my daughter I loved her in the morning as she was leaving for school, and I told her again as I said good night. Twice daily I told each of my sons that I loved him, in the morning and as I said goodnight.

The most surprising thing was that when I said it, I believed it. For those two minutes every day, I really did love all my kids, and that helped to assuage the guilt I felt when I yelled at them, or ignored them because I had no extra energy.

And Babies Make Seven

The tenor of the house changed after I began my two-minute love-in with my kids. I wasn't angry when I told Bryan what had happened and he heard my words without perceiving them as a call to action. He saw the humour, and laughed. The laughter was contagious, and suddenly my life didn't seem so tedious.

Once my counselor and I had my parenting techniques under control, he suggested Bryan and I arrange to go on dates. We needed to nurture our relationship while the passage of time brought change.

Changes were already starting. No longer did babies sit and cry as Bryan arrived home. Now it was a chorus of shrieks and squeals, the patter of feet running towards the back door while four voices tried to say, "Daddy! Daddy! Daddy! Daddy!"

Who would be first in line for a hug from Dad? It re-energized him, and gave me a break to get dinner on the table.

I continued going to counseling sessions until after the boys were in school fulltime, but the meetings were without the rancor and outrage of those first sessions.

I really *was* coping.

17: The Diaper Fiasco

As my composure returned, my husband felt his situation stabilize too. We continued to support each other, but he was glad to return to work in January 1988, after his Christmas vacation.

Meggie was keen to return to Senior Kindergarten after the holiday. She had to walk three blocks to the bus stop, but since her best friend who lived next door went to the same school, they went together. I merely had to make sure she was at our neighbour's house by 8:05 a.m., and her friend's dad walked the two little girls to the bus stop on his way to work. It was an ideal arrangement.

The boys were still going to nursery school, two together, two mornings a week, and several church volunteers, women who'd been helping since the boys' birth, took turns picking them up and driving them. The bus bringing Meggie home from kindergarten dropped her back with us at noon. The volunteer arrived with the two boys at the same time. All five kids were home for the afternoon.

One day in February, I stood at the kitchen sink, looking out the window as Meggie, Geoffrey and Alan tramped up the sidewalk. Richard and Paul were in the family room playing peacefully for a change, Richard with wooden blocks and Paul looking at a picture book.

I'd just finished getting the boys' lunches ready. Four flat-bottomed bowls containing pieces of apple, cheese and bread were waiting on the counter. I turned away from the window, and moved a small plastic table with four small yellow chairs into the kitchen. The set was perfect for our sons. An added bonus was the ease of cleaning. I put it beside the kitchen table where Meggie and I would sit.

As the kids trooped into the house, I helped the boys remove their coats and boots. Meggie took off her own coat while she was telling me about her morning.

"… And what about you, Geoffers? Did you have fun at nursery school?" She asked, using the pet name we had for Geoffrey. She concluded her story by patting her brother on the cheek, but didn't wait for an answer, which wasn't forthcoming anyway. She turned to Alan who was standing quietly, sucking his thumb.

"Oh, Alan!" she said, giving him a quick hug.

I told them to go into the bathroom to wash their hands. (By this time, we had a bathroom downstairs, off the kitchen.) After washing his hands, which in reality meant he held them under running tap water, Geoffrey ran to get his gang-gang, a hand towel he clutched as he sucked his thumb, and he returned to the kitchen.

He wasn't talking yet, but he smiled, showing his dimples, and made a noise that signaled delight as he sat on one of the chairs. Alan, after washing his hands, such as it was, ran to the dining room to find the hat he liked, a red and white train conductor's, and he put it on before taking a seat beside Geoffrey.

Richard and Paul arrived together, at top speed, clutching their gang-gangs. Although Richard wasn't talking yet either, he made sounds as if they were words. Paul tried to talk, and as he sat on a chair, he said, "mum, mum, mum." I grabbed both kids and wiped their hands with a damp washcloth before putting a bowl in front of each boy.

The boys ate with their fingers. It was easier to let them do that than to insist they use utensils. I was confident that eventually they would want to eat with knives and forks, picking up table manners as they grew. Meggie had moved from fingers to flatware by watching Bryan and me.

While the boys played with their food, but ate most of it, Meggie and I munched on sandwiches and carrot sticks. Geoffrey leaned over and took a piece of bread from Alan's bowl, who reciprocated by taking a piece of cheese from his brother's bowl. Then they both stood and shrieked.

I tried to defuse the situation before it erupted into a food fight. "Geoffrey, do you want more bread?"

"Mo' mo' mo'," sang Geoffrey, rocking side to side and stamping his feet. I took this to mean yes, and went to get it.

Richard ate his food carefully and deliberately, as he did most things, singing "la-la-la" softly to himself between bites. Paul "talked" constantly while he ate, but I could only pick out occasional words: "Mum," "Dad," or "Gran-gran"—his name for both my parents.

As the food disappeared, I carried the four training cups half-filled with milk, two at a time, from the counter to the table. I'd learned that to set cups on the table before the boys were ready to drink invited Alan to turn the cup upside down to watch the milk drip. Or maybe this time it would be Richard shaking the cup until the top flew off and the milk exploded onto the floor.

As I sat in the kitchen, absentmindedly listening to Meggie, and watching the boys, I looked at the dining room floor, well-worn hardwood, which until yesterday had been covered with an old, orange carpet. I had disliked it because it made cleaning up after meals extremely difficult. The previous afternoon, after putting the boys in their cribs for a nap, I phoned my neighbour.

"Hi Rita, do you want to bring the kids over and help me redecorate?"

"Sure, Val. What are you planning?"

"I've had it with having to haul the vacuum out to clean after the kids eat. I'm going to rip the carpet out."

"Will Bryan mind?" asked Rita.

"Oh no," I said bravely. "He won't mind. He doesn't like the carpet either."

We did the deed while her two kids and my daughter watched TV in the living room. Since the carpet covered the floors in both rooms, we'd used a utility blade to slice the carpet at the archway.

Despite my brave words, Bryan had been shocked to come home and find the carpet gone except for three pieces under the furniture we couldn't move. After a few days, when he saw how much easier it was to clean the floor, he had to admit it had been a good idea. He did get rid of the three stray pieces though.

The children had finished eating, and I shepherded them to the family room, to change diapers. Lifting Geoffrey to the top of the freezer, I nuzzled him on his cheek. He laughed and batted at my cheek with his hand.

"How's my Geoffers today?" I said laying him on his back.

"Ba-ba-ba," he sang, kicking his heels. When I finished with him, I caught Richard and gave him a hug before laying him on the pseudo change table. After changing his diaper, I put him on the floor with Geoffrey.

Alan and Paul had run back into the living room. I waited a minute, and sure enough, Alan returned, running at top speed. I caught him as he raced by, leaning against the freezer to steady myself.

When I finished with him, Paul was already back, hanging on to my legs, crying. I wasn't sure, but I thought I'd seen him and Geoffrey

177

The Diaper Fiasco

bump into each other as they ran in opposite directions through the kitchen. Paul fell down, started crying, and then crawled to me, but Geoffrey kept going.

These scenes were typical of life in our household for quite a few months. I was very glad each day when Bryan came home and was able to spell me off. Meggie watched Sesame Street or Fred Penner on TV when she was home, giving me a break, but the boys were much more active.

Alan liked to run from the family room through the kitchen to the dining room, wearing a yellow ski hat and his winter boots, yelling all the way. Paul wore his dad's slippers as he rode a riding toy through the kitchen, shrieking with delight as the cat jumped out of his way.

Richard was happier to sit and play with Duplo blocks, frowning in concentration when he slammed them together and they didn't connect. He broke into a radiant smile and laughed when they did, but he screeched in anger if a brother interrupted him.

Geoffrey seemed to be developing a good sense of humour, like his dad. He laughed readily at most mishaps. Since he was slightly bigger than the other three, a collision usually resulted in the other one falling down. At such times his laughter provoked screams and shrieks, which could escalate into a boisterous shoving match.

In the spring of that year, GE Canada asked its employees to work overtime two nights a week to meet production deadlines. This included my husband, which meant that two nights a week I gave the kids their supper and put them to bed. Bryan returned to a mostly quiet house.

One day in May, I was sitting on the back porch, drinking a glass of sherry, when my neighbour's daughter who was my age and who was visiting her mother walked across the street.

"Has it been a hard day?" she said, glancing at the glass.

178

"Bryan is working late again. I've fed the kids, and the boys are in their cribs, ripping wallpaper off the walls. They're laughing and having a great time. Meggie is in bed reading. And I'm here, relaxing, waiting for Bryan to get home."

"Good for you! I don't know how you do it."

"Neither do I sometimes, but it's not like I have a choice." We both laughed and after a few more minutes, she went back to her mom's house.

I sat sipping my sherry, enjoying the warm breeze and early evening calm. When I finished, I went into the house. No sounds from above--that was a good sign. I silently climbed the stairs. Paul was standing in his crib whimpering but the other three were asleep. I went into the bedroom and patted Paul on the back until he settled as well.

I went downstairs, and fifteen minutes later Bryan arrived home. Maybe it was the sherry, or just the fact that the house was peaceful, but after greeting my husband, I broached the topic of taking a holiday, a real holiday, in the summer. Bryan was immediately enthusiastic.

"We could fly to Winnipeg and stay with my aunts, and then rent a van to drive further west," he said with excitement in his voice. "We could stay with friends in Regina, Saskatoon and Red Deer."

"That sounds great!" I said. "It'll be fun to visit and take holidays like normal families do!" We planned to go in July.

The next couple of months passed quickly, as I organized our trip. Everyone I phoned was happy to hear our plans, but again I thought it was a case of the uninitiated being uninformed. It was one thing to talk about having four two-year-olds visit, it was quite another to have them underfoot.

The Diaper Fiasco

We began our journey at the airport in Toronto, and received VIP treatment. The seven of us were driven through the airport on a baggage cart. The jet was still empty when we were shown to our seats.

In planning the trip, we thought to take advantage of free flights for the boys, since they were only two, but we couldn't. We had two children more than adult laps to hold them. Fortunately, we were able to get a seat sale, and paying seven fares ensured that we would have seven meals during the flight.

Since we weren't in the habit of giving our children unnecessary medication, we didn't give them gravol before the flight. This meant that they were all fully awake and ready to go as soon as we were seated.

Bryan loves flying, and was eager to take the boys and Meg, in turn, to the cockpit at the invitation of the flight attendant. (In those pre 911 days, that behaviour was tolerated.)

I wasn't afraid of flying as long as I stayed seated. While Bryan was busy elsewhere, one of the boys ran down the aisle, and I chased after him without realizing what I was doing. I caught up to him several rows back, and had a near panic attack as I realized I was *in the air*, and not on a train or a bus. Very gingerly, I made my way back to my seat and stayed there until we landed.

On the return flight, we medicated the children before we took off, and they slept for most of the flight. At this point, we realized the real benefit of such medicine. It kept *us* calm!

I looked across three sleeping children to the side seats where Bryan was sitting between Meggie, who was resting her head against his arm, and Paul, who was similarly asleep.

"Bry!" I whispered.

He turned to look at me. I gave him a thumbs-up and we both grinned. We were glad to be going home again, after two weeks visiting friends and Bryan's family in cities across the prairies. There had been no major mishaps, and his friends from earlier days had been delighted to see him in his role as the father of five.

On a Saturday morning a few weeks after we'd returned home, I awoke with my mother's intuition on alert. My sixth sense didn't kick in often, but on that morning when I opened my eyes and sensed something was wrong, I woke up instantly.

There was a smell, unfamiliar, yet reminiscent of...vinegar and...tomato as I walked down the back stairs. I stepped into the kitchen, and stopped. The fridge door was open. A broken jar of barbeque sauce was on the floor, hence the smell.

The pitcher of milk, with a deflated bag still in it, was lying in a pool of white. Cheese and chunks of butter, the ketchup bottle (plastic and still intact), unopened beer cans, honey flowing out of its plastic container---a smorgasbord of now inedible eatables were strewn over the floor.

After hearing my exclamation of "Oh dear," Bryan raced down and joined me in the kitchen.

"Good grief!"

"Get the video camera, Bry," I said. "No one will ever believe this!"

Bryan began filming, starting with four pajama-clad boys at the sink in the bathroom on the far side of the kitchen. As I walked across the room, I saw why they were cleaning their hands. The back of the cupboards, which jutted out and separated the back door from the rest of the kitchen, had been finger-painted white with yogurt.

The Diaper Fiasco

After capturing the mess on film and making sure the boys had washed the yogurt off their hands, Bryan took them to the living room to watch cartoons on TV.

I began the clean up, and he returned in minutes to help. I put the unopened beer cans back in the fridge, and realized that the two-litre bottle of wine and the carton of eggs were untouched. We could be thankful for small mercies.

The next day, Bryan bought a bungee cord by which we hooked the front handle to the back of the fridge, making it impossible to open the door without removing the cord first. That would thwart any future attempts at devilry!

In August, we celebrated our sons' third birthday. It was a low-key affair. We invited our daughter's friend from next door, along with her younger brother. Two of our teen-age babysitters also came to help with crowd control.

I made a large slab cake that we divided into four. Meggie decorated one section for each boy. The kids ate at the picnic table in our side yard, leaving crumbs for the birds and squirrels. The animals cleaned up after we had gone back into the house.

With September came my first taste of real freedom—all four boys began attending nursery school together, five afternoons a week. After lunch, I strapped them in the van to drive them. Following that, though, I had two blissful hours all to myself, to do whatever *I* wanted. Since I was out with the van anyway, I often ran errands or bought groceries, but occasionally I visited the library and returned home with a book to read, quietly, and completely alone in the house.

Having those two hours off a day must have triggered latent interests. In a previous life, BC, (Before Children) I'd been concerned about ecological issues. Since the subsequent arrival of my children, I had not had time to indulge that interest. I did what I could, though. At my insistence, the woman who set up the roster of volunteers found someone to take items to the recycling depot once a week.

One day in November, I was feeding the boys their lunch with half an ear tuned to the news on a local radio station. The announcer said that Peterborough city council had sent a letter to the provincial government, asking that plastic diapers be banned, and calling for more research into developing a biodegradable diaper because of the problems the disposable ones posed for landfill sites. As I surveyed my brood, still wearing four or five diapers a day each, I thought of having to go back to using cloth diapers and rubber pants.

The radio announcer continued his report: a local activist, on learning about the city council's plans, was advocating that council begin by banning the diapers completely within our municipality. I thought of the increased washing that such a ban would entail, and I wondered why someone didn't advocate for an ecological alternative to cloth diapers and rubber pants, *before* they restricted the use of disposables.

Giddy with joy at my two hours of freedom a day, I felt called to do something. I phoned an editor whom I knew from writing the columns for the paper several years earlier.

"Banning disposable diapers without having a suitable alternative would be a real hardship for mothers like me," I said.

The editor, sensing a story in the making, asked if she could send a reporter over to take a picture. I agreed, but when the reporter arrived to take the picture, I refused to look at the camera. I gazed down and to my right, at the child sitting beside me.

The next day, my photographer friend at the paper phoned.

"I've just sent the picture of you and the boys out over the wire."

"Oh dear," I said. "I wasn't happy about having that picture taken."

"I could tell," he said, laughing. "There wasn't one picture with you looking at the camera, and I knew you weren't pleased. But it's gone to papers across the country, and I thought I should warn you."

"Thanks." I hung up and immediately phoned Bryan, at work. My husband laughed, but then tried to comfort me by saying maybe nothing would come of it. No such luck!

Two days later another friend phoned to ask if I had looked at the paper yet.

"The letters to the editor page has a Val Keelan corner," he said.

Bryan and I found the paper, lying on the floor, and sure enough, there were two or three letters supporting my claim that just banning disposables was not the answer, and several letters denouncing me for not caring about what happened to the environment.

Over the next couple of months, there were many more letters, some getting personal in supporting or attacking either the activist or me. A couple of months later, when a reporter from a radio station in the US phoned and asked for an interview, it was time to stop the media attention. I had already appeared on a noontime regional TV news show. I'd also been interviewed on a regional radio broadcast. It had been a diversion, but Bryan and I felt the whole episode was blown way out of proportion.

That Christmas, when Bryan was at home for two weeks' holiday, we decided to end the controversy.

"Here are some training pants to wear, Alan. Big boys wear them instead of diapers."

"Bi' boy?"

"Yes, you'll be a big boy now."

I gave the other three training pants as well. We all trooped into the bathroom downstairs so I could show them the toilet.

"Go...go," said Paul.

"Bry, come and get the other guys. Paul says he has to go." I called my husband, who was clearing the lunch table.

After everyone had left–Bryan having to drag Geoffrey away, because he wanted to stay and help–I pulled Paul's pants down and helped him to sit on the toilet seat.

"I'll have to get a stool so you'll be able to sit down by yourself."

"Sit down...self"

"Yes, sit down by yourself."

Paul didn't really have to go, and by the time I had him back together and out of the bathroom Bryan was calling for me to help with Alan and Richard, both of whom had just wet their pants.

And so it went for the two weeks. We let the boys run around without diapers or pants, to give them a greater feeling of having to use the toilet. (And to conserve training pants) With both of us there all day, one was able to tend to accidents while the other maintained order.

By the end of the two-week holiday, two very labour-intensive weeks, three of the boys were mostly reliable, during the day. The fourth boy caught up in another couple of weeks. Still, on the days when everyone had an accident, it called for a lot of patience on my part, not to mention double duty for the washing machine.

Two of the boys stopped wearing diapers at night shortly after going to pants during the day, but the other two used diapers while they slept, for several months. I had discovered a terry cloth diaper, shaped like an hourglass, with Velcro closures and I began using them. They still needed rubber pants, but didn't leak as much. Also there were no pins, to my immense relief.

By year's end, I could see that my family had made great strides forward. My sons had passed one of the first milestones, marking their transition from baby to toddler.

We were a (more or less) happy family unit—a mother, father and five children. As the boys learned to talk, relating to each one was easier. Bryan and I tried to spend time with each child, but it wasn't always possible. He told me about his "50/50 rule." I loved it—a rule, something definite and precise!

"I try to make sure that fifty percent of my interaction with each child is positive," he said.

I decided to adopt it as well, but it didn't always work. Where's the calculator when you need it?

18: Our Own Tiny Tornados

Thinking in terms of fifty-fifty, being diaper-free was both good and bad. On one hand, there wasn't the mess and smell of diapers, but on the other, I was always conscious of four youngsters who, at any moment, might have to tinkle. I left an empty margarine container in the van for several months, in case anyone was caught short. However, one of the benefits of waiting until age three to toilet train a child, as I'd already seen with Meg, was the ability to wait.

It was a good start to the New Year. In the space of a few months, I'd gone from four babies needing diaper changes several times a day, to two guys, only needing diapers at nights.

"Wow," I thought. "Maybe having five children isn't so bad, after all!"

Ha! One February morning, Meg called from her bedroom, "Mum, what are these red spots?"

She was getting dressed while I was in the room down the hall, helping Richard with his clothes.

"Red spots? Let me have a look. Here, Richard, you can put this on yourself." I handed the T-shirt to my son and went to my daughter's room.

"Oh dear, it looks like chicken pox."

"What's that, Mum?" Her face was puckering up, and tears would follow.

187

Our Own Tiny Tornados

"It's not serious, Meg," I reassured her. "It's a disease that kids get. You'll be itchy for a while, but you'll be okay."

My children were hardly ever sick. I had escaped prolonged periods of whiny bad-tempered children thus far, but the appearance of those spots...! All the kids would catch it eventually, and while I knew that simultaneous sickness would mean a quicker end, I dreaded the thought of living with five spotty tots.

I phoned the school to tell them my daughter probably had chicken pox. Later, after dropping the boys off at the nursery school, I took her to the doctor. My diagnosis was confirmed.

When I picked the boys up later, I mentioned that Meg had chicken pox. One of the teachers cautioned me to be on the lookout for spots on the boys. I looked at my sons racing around the room and said, "They don't seem ill now, but the doctor said kids with chicken pox often don't act sick."

The teacher smiled and said, "I don't envy you being home with five sick children!"

I was not looking forward to it either, but my morning routine expanded to include checking each child for spots. Two days later, Richard showed signs of a rash, and I took him to the doctor. It turned out to be a viral skin infection, but I opted to keep him home in expectation that it would develop into the pox, which it did.

Since the disease is most contagious at its outset, Bryan and I decided it would be best to keep all the kids home and let it run its course.

"In some ways," I told him one evening, "it's easier to keep everyone at home than to be trying to get some of them ready for school while the others get to stay home."

"They don't 'get to stay home.' They're sick, and *have* to stay home."

"That's not how they see it. Look at Richard. He doesn't act sick. The other guys figure he's 'getting' to stay home."

Bryan rolled his eyes and laughed. "I'm glad I go to work. I'll let you deal with this."

"Thanks." I said, but I was laughing too.

My mother came to help for a few days while Meg was bedridden. I needed the extra hands to tend her while I kept the household going. Meg was spot-free and able to return to school a week later. After four days of school, it was March break, and my parents took her to their place for a week.

Meanwhile, I was confined to the house with four spotted boys. Richard had pox inside his mouth and all over his head. His hair was quite long, making it difficult to apply calamine lotion. I phoned the hairdressing salon. The woman who cut my hair had already had the disease, and she was able to come to my house to cut his hair.

The sickness only slowed my sons down marginally. I had had visions of the five of us watching videos together, or me reading a book to them, sitting quietly on the couch. In my dreams!

However, one day two of them did slow down and Alan hugged Richard, exclaiming, "You my best friend!"

"Isn't that sweet," I thought, watching them. They looked so cute, two little boys, standing and hugging each other. "Maybe because they *have* to stay home together, they won't fight as much."

"Yes, and maybe pigs will fly," I thought later when I saw Richard swipe a toy from Alan who hurled the ultimate insult, "You not my best friend anymore!"

Our Own Tiny Tornados

We had only one cat at this time, the other having succumbed to old age a few years previously. Alan was intrigued at the cat's method of eating. When Paul spilled his cup of orange juice while carrying it to the table, Alan, who was following him, got down on his hands and knees to slurp it up.

After seeing that I thought, "Some women are proud of houses so clean you can 'eat off the floor.' Now I can boast that even though my house isn't clean, someone *has* eaten off the floor!"

I survived the six-week springtime pox infection. Several friends who didn't mind being exposed to the disease babysat for me so I could go out to shop, or escape the pandemonium with a cup of tea at a neighbour's house. I was very glad that modern medicine had discovered vaccines to prevent the occurrence of other childhood diseases.

Our sons were a medical anomaly, and the only set of quadruplets in the city. Their birth had received media attention, and many people knew our name. When people met my sons for the first time, they would often ask, "Which one are you?"

Conversely, when we were out and met someone I knew, I would instruct the boys, "Tell (whomever) what your name is."

All this attention to names made an impact on Geoffrey. When the women who cleaned our house arrived, he ran to the door and asked, "What your name?"

If I stopped to talk to acquaintances in the mall, my son would gaze up at them and ask his most important question, "What your name?"

If Geoffrey asked a total stranger whose name he had no need to know, I tried to change the topic quickly, or to shift his interest to something else. Overall people were very understanding, however, smiling and saying, 'Jim' or 'Mary' or whatever.

190

And Babies Make Seven

The boys were three and a half years old. Even though they were getting in and out of their cribs on their own, Bryan and I felt it was time to switch them to proper beds. We had been delaying this, wondering how we were going to afford to buy four beds.

It turned out we didn't have to. My aunt and uncle, who had raised five sons of their own, had two single-size box spring and mattresses, and two single-size wooden bed frames that were still useable. They offered them to us.

We set the wooden frames in one bedroom, and put the mattresses on them for two boys. The other two boys slept on the box springs in the other room. Since the boys constantly changed bedrooms and sleeping companions, depending on who was getting along with whom at any given time, we didn't think that sleeping on a box spring would be harmful, at least for a few years, until we could buy better beds.

With the boys sleeping in regular beds, it was easier for them to get out, but Bryan and I had strictly enforced a definite bedtime with our daughter, and we continued to impose the rule after our increase in progeny.

"You can talk, but you have to stay in your beds," we told our sons. Since there were two boys in each bedroom, it was unrealistic to expect total silence as soon as they climbed into bed. As long as they remained in their beds, we ignored the muted (or occasionally louder) mutterings.

One morning in July, I had a chance to put into practice a parenting principle learned the previous year. That morning, one of my sons refused to get dressed. Several requests of 'Please get dressed' were met with a 'No!' or were simply ignored altogether. When it was time to drive them to the day care they were attending, I took his clothes and shoes, put him in the van with the other boys who were dressed, and drove across town. (The boys went daily for two weeks, a gift from a local social service agency.)

When I took the children in, I apologized to the head teacher. She waved my apology aside as she accepted the bag of clothes and the pair of shoes.

"Don't worry, Mrs. Keelan," she said while smiling at my son in his pyjamas. I left, but when I returned two hours later, all were dressed. Refusal to get dressed was never a problem, after that.

One Saturday morning, I was enjoying a solitary cup of tea and doing a crossword puzzle, a rare luxury for me. Bryan had taken the four boys out while he did some errands, and Meg was visiting a friend. I heard the car pull into the driveway, and I knew I'd lost the chance to finish the word game.

"Hi guys! Did you have a good time?"

"Nooo," sobbed Geoffrey. "I want to sit in the front."

"You wanted to sit in the front and you couldn't?" I asked.

"He didn't like having to take his turn, but everyone had to." Bryan said through gritted teeth, putting the bags he was carrying on the counter. I sensed his frustration—it was radiating off him in waves.

I ushered the guys into the house, and took them into the living room. I turned the TV on, and wiped Geoffrey's nose. He was happier now, watching The Smurfs. Two boys climbed onto the couch, and two stretched out on the floor. Satisfied that they were happy and involved in what was happening on the screen, I returned to the kitchen, where Bryan was making a cup of coffee.

"Was it difficult this morning?" I asked, resuming my seat at the table, and refilling my cup.

"When we left, everyone wanted to sit in the front," Bryan explained. He had taken the Beamer for the drive around town. We didn't like to use the van unless we were doing highway driving now that the boys were old enough that they didn't need car seats.

"How did you decide who sits where? When you take Meg, I know you let her sit in the front because she's the oldest."

"I said Geoffrey could sit in the front until the first stop. I was using GARP order." Bryan said. "After we stopped the first time, I said it was Alan's turn. Then after the second stop, Richard's, and after the last stop Paul's."

"So Geoffrey's been crying almost the whole time? Because he couldn't sit in the front?"

"Not really. He went along with it until we were on our way home. Then he turned on the tears again just before we got home." Bryan had calmed down, and as he set his mug on the table, he started to laugh. "He must've thought you'd take his side if he was crying!"

"Oh dear. Poor Geoffers." I looked towards the living room. "Well, he seems over it now. I'll see if he wants a snack. Maybe he was hungry."

Geoffrey did want a snack, but once I mentioned it, everyone else wanted one too. Bryan was finishing his coffee when I entered the kitchen.

I took four graham crackers from the box and handed them to Bryan. "Take these to the guys, and give Geoffrey a hug."

"Woof, woof," said Bryan, taking the biscuits and heading towards the sounds of the boys laughing.

I smiled. Bryan always pretended he was a trained dog when I told him to do something. I looked at our cups on the table. My tea was cold. I dumped it out and put the dishes in the dishwasher.

Our Own Tiny Tornados

That afternoon we tried taking the boys for their first real haircut. Bryan opened the door and I guided the four boys into the barbershop. The barber was cutting one man's hair, and another was waiting.

"Here, Geoffrey and Alan, come and sit with me," I said, sitting on one of the two remaining chairs.

They came to me, each with his thumb in his mouth, and leaned against me.

"How many?" asked the barber.

"Just the boys," said Bryan. The barber reached over and flicked four switches, and four more green lights glowed at the top of the window.

The barber switched the TV to a cartoon show and the four boys sat on the floor, faces turned to the screen. I looked at him and smiled my thanks.

After ten minutes, it was our turn.

"Here, Alan, do you want to sit in the big chair?" Bryan grabbed his hand and pulled him towards it.

"Nooooo." Alan straightened his legs and leaned back.

"It's all right, Alan. I'll stay here with you. Look, the barber's putting in a bench for you to sit on." Bryan lifted him into the chair. Alan caught sight of his reflection in the mirror, and stopped crying.

As the barber tied a cape around him, Richard crossed the floor to stand beside the chair and he looked up at his brother. His face turned from Alan's to the reflection and he pointed to the mirror, saying his brother's name.

Alan tolerated having the barber take a few snips from the hair at the back of his head, but then he started wiggling and turning his head.

"I'm sorry," said Bryan as he lifted his son out of the chair. Another customer had entered. The barber switched off three of the lights.

And Babies Make Seven

We apologized again as we left. I continued to trim the boys' hair when it was necessary. It was another year before we tried going again. By then the boys were happy to sit in the big chair.

When we returned home, Bryan set a video going, and came into the kitchen to help prepare dinner. After we ate, the boys spent an hour in the yard, running off steam. Then Bryan took them upstairs to give them a bath, which was followed by story time.

While Bryan was occupied with the children, I tidied the kitchen. It gave me time to think. After having attended nursery school for more than a year and the day care earlier in the summer, the boys were used to schedules. I continued the routine at home, by pretending to run my own small day care.

Some days our activity time involved playing in the wading pool, inside our fenced side yard. On other days, the four boys each rode his trike around the block, and I accompanied them. After we returned home, we'd have snack time, and then we'd enjoy quiet time while my children watched TV or read picture books. (I might have enjoyed it more than they did!)

I finished putting the dishes in the dishwasher, and set it going. While wiping the counters, I thought back to my last grocery trip. I had asked a teenager who babysat for us to come too.

While I had collected groceries in one cart, she pushed the four boys in another. I heard them discussing the foods on the shelves, who liked what and whether they liked the pictures on the boxes, as they went up one aisle and down the next.

When Bryan came downstairs, I went to the boys' bedrooms to say goodnight. Three of the boys settled immediately, but Paul wanted me to stay with him until he fell asleep. I sat on the floor, leaning against his bed, prepared for a silent count to three hundred. He was asleep before the five minutes had passed.

In August, the boys celebrated their fourth birthday. Since it fell on a Sunday, it was the perfect opportunity to spend the weekend at Granny and Grandpa's. We could have a party there and share the wealth. Why should we limit the fun of four four-year olds revved on sugar to just the parents?

Our sons' behaviour was the same, no matter whom we visited. The four of them created a constant whirlwind. We travelled with our own tiny tornados. They fed on each other's energy, causing confusion wherever they went. Papers in piles were transformed into scattering swirls of sheets. Toys were dropped anywhere as a toddler's interest transferred to another. My mother tried unsuccessfully to keep eight sticky hands and forty jam-smeared fingers clean.

Back home after that brief visit, it was easier to redirect the energy into positive action, such as Dad's Saturday morning coffee. One person put the sugar in, and another person (usually Meg) poured the milk. Someone else stirred. Yikes, two people without tasks! Quick, think of something!

Find the paper so Paul can take it to Dad. Richard can take him his slippers. Calamity diverted! Everyone felt useful. Finally, the summer was over, and our schedule shifted again.

Starting in September 1989, all five kids caught the bus in the morning. Meg was in Grade 2, and the boys attended Senior Kindergarten for a half day. They were bussed home at noon, but I had to have four sandwiches ready. We had one hour to eat before I took them to nursery school.

And Babies Make Seven

After dropping them off, I had two more hours to myself, before picking them up and taking them home again.

I rarely did housework during my time off, since cleaning the house was not high on my list of priorities. Bryan and I didn't object to seeing dust bunnies or even dust elephants. It wasn't surprising, therefore, to overhear Alan one day, saying, "There's a 'pider."

He got down on his hands and knees to watch it cross the kitchen floor, and his brothers joined him. Four of them, crowded around this poor defenseless spider-I pitied the arachnid!

Paul sat back on his haunches and clapped his hands, exclaiming, "It's not a big, fat spider. It's a nice little spider."

The four of them continued to watch it making its way towards the family room.

"It going to clean the house, right?" Geoffrey asked Meg, who was walking by.

"Spiders eat bugs," affirmed Meg, the self-proclaimed authority on all matters of interest.

Paul pointed to the rug in the family room and asked, "Are there spiders under there? Will they clean the basement?"

Meg had gone upstairs, having delivered her opinion on the subject. Paul's question remained unanswered. He joined Richard playing with Lego in the family room. The spider had disappeared. It was no longer relevant.

Cleaning house was not an activity I enjoyed, and neither was sewing. I was very pleased, therefore, when my mother announced she would make four Halloween costumes. That year we had two four-year-old Spider Man(s), and two four-year-old Batman(s). The boys struck fearsome poses, but the whole effect was washed out as it rained for the entire evening, and we had to return home after visiting only a few houses. We were able to use the costumes for the next couple of years, however.

Bryan and I went out for dinner on December 1, to celebrate my thirty-seventh birthday. During dessert, he reminded me he would have two weeks off at Christmas since he hadn't used all his summer vacation days.

"That's good. We'll be able to do our Christmas shopping while the kids are at school."

Bryan's father and his two aunts had sent money to buy toys for the kids, as they had in other years, rather than trying to send presents in the mail. After Bryan began his holidays, we spent an afternoon buying dolls and books for Meg, Lego for Richard, and an assortment of other toys. Alan liked toys with moveable parts and buttons he could push. Geoffrey liked books, (The Berenstain Bears series was always a favourite) and Lego or other blocks. Paul liked books too, and Lego, and riding toys. Each child had his own presents to open, but after that, the toys were fair game for everyone.

More toys to store, the children growing…we needed more room. Also, since they liked to play outdoors, it was time to move to a quieter neighbourhood. Bryan and I spent that summer and fall viewing houses for sale.

This was another 'big production' time…we had to call in our regular babysitter, a teenage girl who lived nearby, to stay with the children while we looked at houses. This meant scheduling the visits in advance—no impulse buying for us!

After a couple of months, we found another house we liked. Our offer to purchase was contingent on selling our house.

We had listed it with an agent who, besides selling real estate, also worked at CGE with Bryan. Our agent was a friend who was familiar with our particular situation, and she did double duty trying to sell our house. She actually came over to vacuum and help tidy prior to open houses! But as the year ended, we had no takers.

In the same way that we couldn't run out to look at houses on a whim, so also we couldn't have prospective buyers stopping in to look at our house without warning. How appealing is it to view a house with toys scattered from one end to the other?

"Maybe the reason no one wants to buy our house is because there's so much junk all over the place. Look at all these toys the kids never play with any more, and those bags of clothes don't fit the kids any longer." I turned around and pointed to the green garbage bag in the opposite corner. "Those clothes will fit the kids in the next few months."

"I know, Val. It's frustrating, not having any interest in this house, when we've already picked one out," my husband replied. "Maybe it's a slow market. I'll see if we can renew our offer for another three months."

The homeowner in the suburbs was not willing to renew our offer again. Our real estate agent, our very accommodating agent, took boxes and bags of toys and clothes to her house, until we could find a buyer.

Meanwhile, besides trying to sell our house and buy another, we had December activities to keep us busy. We attended school Christmas concerts and parties. Bryan accompanied us to the Christmas Eve service, to watch the children in another concert. On Christmas morning, Meg roused her brothers at 5:30, and the five of them emptied their Santa stockings before dragging their parents downstairs.

Our Own Tiny Tornados

Granny Jean and Grandpa Tony arrived Christmas afternoon, and we had another unwrapping session. Bryan was able to cook the Christmas turkey, and we all enjoyed his culinary efforts.

As the holidays ended, our visitors left and our regular life resumed. Our tiny twisters had nine months left to spin before school capped their energy.

We finally had a buyer for our house. Let's find one to buy!

19: Mary Poppins and the Superb System

Bryan and I spent the first two weeks of January, researching houses for sale. I wanted a newer house, one that had more storage space and was easy to clean. I wanted to live in a nice neighbourhood, but not on a hill. However, other than that I wasn't fussy.

Bryan liked older homes, with nooks, crannies, and charm. Already we were at cross-purposes, but, as with other situations in which we'd disagreed, we began discussing and negotiating.

What did we each like and dislike about the houses? Which were in neighbourhoods we wanted? Which locations allowed the children to stay in the same school? Eventually we found one we both liked. Or rather, that I liked and that Bryan liked well enough to overlook the parts he didn't, to keep peace in our marriage.

It was a recently built, open-concept house. After we moved in, I was pleased to be able to work in the kitchen and oversee the kids in the family room. The yard was not completely finished, giving Bryan a chance to try his hand at landscaping.

However, the real benefit of the house was having four decent sized bedrooms. One on the main floor was small, but suitable for our eight-year-old daughter. She liked having a bathroom directly opposite.

Upstairs were two bedrooms, each a good size, plus the master bedroom. We put two beds in one room, plus a dresser, and the same in the other room, for our four sons. And that's when the bickering began!

Mary Poppins and the Superb System

Alan wanted to sleep with Richard who wanted to sleep with Geoffrey who wanted to sleep with Paul who wanted to sleep with Alan. We flipped coins, drew straws, made promises, (if you sleep with a brother you don't want to tonight, tomorrow you can sleep with the brother you do…) trying to decide who would sleep where. However, by the next night, different brothers wanted to sleep together.

I could not deal with it. My stomach ached and my neck hurt. I was overwrought and distraught. Fortunately, Bryan was decisive enough to deal with the kerfuffle. He also had a surefire way of getting the process started.

"It's bedtime. First one upstairs and in his pyjamas can sit next to me while I read the story." He was reading Tolkien's "The Hobbit." They all gathered in one bedroom for the story, and at its end two boys went into the other bedroom to sleep. But which two? While they came to that decision, I tidied the kitchen, made Bryan's lunch, loaded the dishwasher and set it going. I did *anything* to block out the sounds of discord!

After they arrived at a suitable arrangement, I went into each bedroom for my nightly 'I love you.' Doing so was no longer necessary for my emotional well-being, but saying it had become a habit.

One night, when they were seven years old, one of my sons said, "I know you do, Mum, you tell us every night." It had served its purpose, and I could stop.

The boys were growing and Bryan and I knew the cast-off beds from my aunt and uncle would soon be unsuitable. A couple of years after moving, we bought two sets of bunk beds and put them in one of the upstairs rooms, against one wall and side by side. It was a double bunk, but with two sets of sheets on each level. This reduced the nighttime

202

bickering, but increased the party aspect of bedtime with an hour, at least, of talking before sleep.

Our daughter moved to the other upstairs bedroom. Having a bathroom nearby had lost its appeal, and since everyone else was sleeping on the second floor, she said she felt "lonely."

This sleeping arrangement freed a room on the main floor. We moved the computer out of the master bedroom and into the empty room at the back of the house. (It had been in the master bedroom to limit access from four industrious lads who knew exactly how much tape an ink cartridge held!)

Our computer had been upgraded from the one Bryan had built in 1985, to a faster one. Over the years, as the children wanted to use computers for games and school, he developed a system for obtaining workable ones at an affordable cost.

He bought a middle-of-the-road model, and used it for two years. By then newer systems that were faster and less expensive were available. An upgrade was deemed necessary, (for the children of course) and various parts were purchased. The discarded components were stored, and as this cycle was repeated over the years, they were used in other machines, giving us "first grade" and "second grade" computers.

Bryan used available network technology to link them, giving us our own LAN. (Local Area Network) Through it, the two computers the children used in the family room, and the one in the living room that he and I used, were able to talk to each other.

To distinguish between the three computers, since we had two in one room, the children named them: Fast Eddy (it was a joke, this one was actually the slowest), Little John (because it had less memory), and

203

Mary Poppins and the Superb System

Athena, in the living room. In Greek mythology, Athena was goddess of wisdom, a fitting name for the best computer in the system.

The boys liked playing computer games. Three of them stood around the table, cheering on the boy working the controls. However, after a while, one of the observers felt it should be his turn to play. The transition was not always smooth.

As the rough passages intensified, I was glad they were in the back room. I tried to pretend I was deaf, but it did not always work. One day I was peeling potatoes in the kitchen. Geoff ran into the family room.

"Mum, Alan won't let me play."

"It's not his turn," called Alan from the back room.

"Alan, how long have you been playing?" I asked reasonably, only loud enough to carry into the back room.

"Not long."

"It's been a long time," Geoff exclaimed.

"I'm not finished my game," wailed Alan.

"Aha," I thought. "The crux of the matter!"

"How long will it take to finish your game?" I called, "Half an hour? Five minutes? Ten minutes?"

"I don't know." Alan shouted back.

"All right," I said, walking through the family room. "I'm going to set the oven timer for ten minutes. When you hear it buzzing, I want you to let Geoff play. You and your brothers can watch. I'll reset it, and then Richard can have a turn while the rest of you watch. Then I'll reset it for Paul's turn. That way you can each have a turn playing."

GARP order, to the rescue!

Alan grumbled a bit more, but finally said, "O.K., Mum. I guess that'll work."

And Babies Make Seven

Personally, I thought it was a great idea, and relieved me from watching the clock to make sure each child only had ten minutes playing time. After a few months, the guys liked it so much they'd tell me themselves to set the timer. Score one for Mum!

When we'd first moved into our house, the large family room housed the TV and a couch, leaving lots of room for running around, or having a "party" with the stuffed animals, or launching paper airplanes, or doing a host of other activities kids might find entertaining, like squabbling.

I knew that childhood disagreements were normal, and all siblings quarreled. At the same time, I felt that if I were a perfect mother, a present day Mary Poppins, my children would spend their days in blissful harmony, cheering each other on and reveling in each other's company. All I needed was a Superb System.

"That's the ticket," I thought, "having fun with my kids, playing games while tidying. 'Supercalifragilisticexpialidocious'; 'Just a spoonful of sugar'…" That could be me!

I had each boy pick a corner of our spacious family room. A half hour later, when the bickering became unbearable, I mentally clicked my heels and adopted my MP persona. I clapped my hands and called out, "to your corners!"

Each boy raced to his corner and the arguing stopped. This was great! It would be my lifeline-the kids would never argue again.

When I tried to use the same tactic the next day, however, two boys forgot which corner was theirs, and raced to the same one. As they started hitting each other, I yelled, "Stop it! Stop it right now!"

My MP persona was dented, but not broken. After shooing everybody outside and making myself a cup of tea, I conjured up a vision of Mary Poppins. She would not let one failure defeat her. She would click her heels, twirl her umbrella and think again.

My alliterative mind came up with the three C's: Co-operation, Consideration, and Compromise. I would encourage my children to co-operate with each other, be considerate of one other's feelings, and compromise to find solutions. *That* would reduce the argy-bargy that led to fights!

"I'll write the words on a piece of paper and tape it to the wall," I thought. Before doing it however, reality hit. Why did I think having a poster on the wall was going to influence my children's behaviour?

("You stupid jerk; it's not your turn." "Yes it is, you moron." "Oh look at the writing on the wall—Mum wants us to co-operate, be considerate and use compromise." "Oh I say; why don't you go first?" "No, no, you go first...I insist." "No, no you go first.")

Yeah, right. As if...

The kids and I limped through to September, and the boys started grade one. The end of the tunnel! All the children were out of the house for eight hours a day, and I no longer felt my husband's work place was a vacation in disguise.

A month after we'd moved, Bryan had transferred from GE Canada to Ontario Hydro. As a GE employee, he had been on loan to the Darlington Nuclear Power Plant, assisting Ontario Hydro to install the software he had helped write in the preceding years.

The transfer meant the source of his paycheck changed, but the actual work stayed the same. As a new Hydro employee, however, he had to take a training course for several weeks.

And Babies Make Seven

The course required that Bryan work a 12-hour shift, which meant he didn't arrive home until after the boys' bedtime. I had to forego my kitchen chores, and endure the nightly sleeping partner selection process.

I was glad when Bryan finished the training and resumed his regular hours. He continued the nightly consensus reaching ritual, and once again, I stayed out of it. I had to be in tip-top form twelve hours later. The mornings were my domain.

It was good planning on Bryan's part, I thought, to leave the house at 6:45 a.m., before the rest of us were up. Eventually, however, our routine had become so tightly choreographed that if Bryan was home from work on a school day, I asked him to stay in bed until everyone was out the door. Then he could come downstairs and wave good-bye to the kids.

Three years after moving to the house in the suburbs, the boys were in grade four, Meg was in grade seven, and our morning routine was firmly entrenched. I got up as Bryan was leaving the house, at 6:45 a.m..

I went into one bedroom, turned on the light, and waited for an indication the boys were stirring: grunts and stretches. Next, I flicked the switch in another bedroom. Similar noises and actions greeted the illumination. I progressed to my daughter's room.

I pressed the on button of the radio on her bedside table, and heard The Guess Who, singing 'These Eyes.' It took me back to my teenage years, listening to records with my boyfriend. That had been a hit song then, and we'd played it for hours. Meg's grumbled "Go away" quickly brought me back to the present. She wasn't a morning person, and not even listening to 'golden oldies' was going to change her.

"Come on, Meg. It's time to get up. Are you awake?"

"Yes." Her voice was muffled, but she was stirring.

Mary Poppins and the Superb System

I descended the stairs and spotted Alan, with his pants and sweater grasped in a bundle, sitting on top of the heater vent in the living room.

"Why is it so cold in here, Mum?"

"It's October, and winter is coming. After you're dressed you won't notice it."

Richard appeared in the front room, clutching his clothes, and he claimed the other heater by the front window.

"Hey Alan, do you want to hear what bear-bear did last night?" He asked, while starting to get dressed.

"Sure," said Alan although it was somewhat muffled as he pulled his top over his head.

I tuned them out as I started to get the sandwiches ready. At age nine, they still liked to talk about their stuffed animals, making up stories about what they did and where they went. I couldn't listen. I had to keep my mind on what I was doing.

Alan wanted peanut butter and grape jelly on brown bread while Paul wanted peanut butter and honey on white. I put two slices of white bread on the counter and two slices of brown. After spreading peanut butter on all slices, I had to stop and think – grape on brown, honey on white. Heaven help me if I made a mistake!

My other two sons' lunches were dissimilar enough that I didn't have to concentrate as much. Meg's lunch varied. I filled drink containers until she came downstairs and put in her order.

Making lunches, I could handle. Trying to keep track of who wanted what for a snack, I couldn't. My first 'morning routine rule' was established: Each person is responsible for getting his or her own snacks. To make it easy for them to do this when they were small, I kept the food they used as snacks–cereal, crackers, and granola bars, as well as containers, in floor level cupboards.

My second rule for the morning was that if someone was sick and couldn't go to school, they had to stay in bed until after the others had left.

If a child was able to nag me, insisting that he or she wasn't well enough to go to school, the child probably was. Someone who really was sick stayed in bed.

I had to keep my wits about me to get the correct lunch into the proper lunch bag. I lined them up in GARP order on the kitchen counter, with Meg's at the end, ready for the kids to put in their own snacks. After doing that, they closed the bags.

As they raced by me to the mudroom for their hats and coats before going out through the garage, I gave each of them a one-armed hug. I counted in my head: one…two…three…four…five.

With the house to myself at last, I was able to enjoy a cup of tea, and relax for a few minutes. I contemplated how my life had changed over the years. Sure, those early years had been hectic, but there had been a certain order to it. Babies are unable to look after themselves, and everything is done for them. My job, back then, had been very specific. When a baby cries, discover the reason and fix the problem. Thinking back, it had all been so easy!

"Yeah, right," I thought. "But the babies had become children,"

We loved our children, and were grateful all of them were bright and inquisitive. However, questioning on their part had involved answering on our part, and giving replies to the boys' questions had taken a special kind of patience.

"Dad, whatcha doin'?"

209

Mary Poppins and the Superb System

The Christmas after we'd moved had been the first year we'd been able to put decorative lights on our house, and Bryan, who was always happy to explain his actions, told the boy who was standing at the foot of the ladder and out of his line of sight, that he was putting up Christmas lights. He was fastening them to the eaves trough.

"Hi Dad. What are ya doing?"

Bryan launched into his explanation again, shortening it somewhat.

The third time a voice asked the question, Bryan answered as patiently as he could but by the fourth time Bryan snapped, "Look, I've already told you…" when he stopped and took a second to reflect. That hadn't been one boy asking the same thing over and over. It had actually been four different voices!

Questions to me were different. It was Saturday, and I was making lunch for my six-year-old sons.

"Mum, what comes after 'R'?"

"Mum, what else begins with 'P'?"

"Mum, is there an 'A' in peanut butter?"

"Mum, is there a 'G' in peanut butter?"

Spreading peanut butter on eight slices of bread, I had to remember that Richard was spelling his name, Paul was listing his favourite foods that began with the letter P, and Alan and Geoff were figuring out which of their favourite foods had the same letters as their names. I paused a moment to think.

"i, peanut butter, yes, no," I said, correctly answering each question, and opening a jar to finish making PB & J sandwiches. And I'd wondered if I'd be able to listen to four conversations at once. Piece of cake!

I stopped daydreaming and put my mug in the dishwasher. Taking the dog's leash from the hook by the door, I asked, "Moses, do you want to go for a walk?"

Figure 22: Moses

In answer, he pranced around, making it hard to clip his leash. After a few fumbles, we were ready.

As we walked around the block, I recalled the afternoon, shortly after we'd moved, that my mother and I had been finishing our lunch, sitting in the kitchen.

She had come to stay with me for a few days after I'd had a hysterectomy. The boys had gone to Senior Kindergarten in the morning, and were home for the afternoon. They were watching a cartoon on TV, but I gradually realized they were laughing at more than the show. I leaned to the left to look past my mother, through the railing, and into the family room.

"Oh no, look what they've done. Bryan is going to be furious!"

Mom turned around. "Oh my goodness!"

Our beautiful umbrella plant, once lush and leafy, was a spindly stem with only one or two leaves still attached. My mother started gathering up those on the floor, to take outside.

"Guys," I said. "Dad is not going to like this."

They had been unconcerned, and had turned their attention back to the TV show. When Bryan came home from work, I'd tried to prepare him for the shock of seeing the once prolific plant reduced to a single, nearly bare, stalk.

"We had a problem this afternoon..."

"Uh-oh, what happened?" Bryan hung his jacket in the hall and walked into the kitchen. I pointed.

He was still as his gaze followed my finger. I could see the emotions cross his face. Dismay...anger...the urge to do bodily harm...but he swallowed and collected himself.

"Guys, this is not good," he said, tersely. Geoff was laughing at something on the TV. Richard was waving his bear-bear around. Paul and Alan ran across the room, yelling "Daddy, Daddy!"

"Oh well," he said, squatting to catch Paul and Alan in a hug. "Maybe it'll grow back."

It had done just that. The leaves had grown to be more plentiful than before, making the plant look even better. Thereafter we talked about how they had pruned the plant, not that they'd stripped the leaves!

And Babies Make Seven

Returning from my walk with the dog, I assembled the vacuum cleaner. I'd decided that since the kids were out of the house during school hours, I would have time to clean the house. (It was true, but the inclination was still a little weak!) Still, in the interests of saving money, I vacuumed.

When I finished vacuuming the family room and the downstairs bedroom, I hauled the vacuum upstairs. The double bunks in one room had lasted a few years, but we'd ended the camp-like atmosphere two years after we'd moved. The main floor study had been converted back to a bedroom, with two single beds and a dresser. I'd noted when I was downstairs that it didn't take long to vacuum–it was small to begin with, and furniture covered most of the floor space.

With the decision to separate the four boys, suddenly my stomach pains, sore neck and headaches returned. Mary Poppins resurfaced. There must be a way to resolve this! My love of schedules prompted me to suggest writing a roster of who sleeps where each night, but…

"That won't work," Geoff informed me. "I might not want to sleep with Richard one night, and if the schedule says I have to…it won't work."

"And I won't want to sleep with you," Richard muttered, not wanting to be outdone.

"Then we can go back to flipping coins every night," Bryan suggested. "Here Geoff, heads or tails?"

On occasion, not even flipping a coin produced satisfactory results. The pairing would be Geoff and Paul, Richard and Alan, but Alan and Geoffrey really, really, really wanted to sleep together because they had been playing a game, and wanted to continue their discussion in their beds. But there was "no way" Richard would sleep with Paul…it was a never-ending battle.

Mary Poppins and the Superb System

To complicate matters, no one wanted to sleep in the bedroom on the main floor. Because of that, the boys thought that whoever agreed to sleep there should be able to choose his sleeping partner. However, if that brother didn't want to sleep with him…no wonder I was going grey at an alarming rate!

Finally, in 1997, I would put my foot down. Mary Poppins be damned! I was fed up and was not going to take this anymore! At that time, I would issue a proclamation:

"From now on, Geoff and Alan will always sleep in the downstairs bedroom. Richard and Paul will always sleep in the upstairs bedroom."

Once stated, it became law, and was deemed fair. Geoff and Alan had similar sleep patterns, as had Richard and Paul, so unknowingly I had picked a good pairing, perhaps even the best. (MP must have influenced me.)

I finished vacuuming upstairs and lugged the machine back to the first floor. I returned it to its storage corner, and went back upstairs to fetch the laundry baskets from my bedroom.

It was washday. Every other day was, in fact. I could have done smaller loads every day, but I was perverse enough to want two or three days a week without doing laundry. Gathering all the dirty clothes, I took them to the basement to begin sorting. Looking at the clothes, I thought again about my sons.

We had rarely dressed the boys in similar outfits. When asked about this when they were newborns, Bryan had laughed as he explained, "Can you imagine having them in identical outfits and every time one of them spits up we'd have to change all four?"

Having all the tops in one dresser drawer and all the pants in another was fine while the clothes were small. After we moved, however, the boys were older and the clothes bigger. I put tops of one size in one drawer and pants in another. In another dresser were tops and pants of a larger size.

The next step was to give each boy his own dresser. Once we did that, it was my job to put the correct clothes in the proper dresser. I soon recognized which clothes fit which boys. Although very few clothes belonged to only one boy, there were exceptions. And since I wasn't perfect, sometimes I goofed. I recalled the other morning.

"Alan, take that top off. It's mine!" Richard had yelled, seeing his brother coming down the stairs.

"No, I can wear it. It was in my dresser."

"But it's my top, that's the one my godparents gave me! You can't wear it! Mum, tell Alan he can't wear my top!"

Looking at it more closely, I recognized it as the one my friend had sent to Richard for his birthday.

"Oh, I'm sorry, Al. It *is* Rick's shirt. I should've known that. I put it in the wrong drawer. Do you mind changing?"

"I guess not, but it *was* in my drawer." Alan turned around and headed back upstairs to change.

Having finished with the laundry for the moment, I went to the kitchen to make myself a sandwich and a cup of tea for lunch. While I ate, my thoughts went back a few years.

One morning, the year after we moved, there had been only one granola bar left, and the kids had decided it would be for Daddy. The next morning, Geoff and Al were in the kitchen before their brothers, and they both wanted it. They had decided to share it, when Richard and Paul entered the room and seeing the other two about to open the packaging, they both yelled, "That's for Dad!"

215

Geoff and Alan immediately said, "Oh yeah" and returned in to the box.

"Amazing!" I thought as I'd watched the scenario unfold. "Maybe being multiples they have a stronger sense of fairness."

I also remembered another day as I was taking Geoffrey, Alan, Richard and Paul out in the van. I had just pulled out of the driveway when Paul called out, "Mum, stop the van. I don't want my brother to go to jail. Geoff, do your seat belt up!"

I pulled to the curb while we resolved things. Richard didn't want Geoff to sit between him and Alan on a front bench. Geoff had gone to the back of the van, refusing to put his belt on because he didn't want to sit on the other side of Richard.

It took a few minutes of talking back and forth before Geoff found a suitable seat and both he and Richard were happy. Then everyone fastened seat belts and we were able to continue. There was a bond among the four of them that I'm not sure Bryan or I, or even Meg, ever fully understood.

This bond had an inherent pecking order, I had learned, when I overheard them discussing the family ranking: "Dad's the boss. What he says goes. When's he's not here, Mum is the boss. When she's not here, Meg is the boss. When she's not here, Geoff is the boss and when he's not here, Richard is the boss."

The question of the pecking order between Alan and Paul alone was not answered; either they couldn't imagine only those two being here, or if it were just them, they didn't think they needed a boss.

I finished my sandwich and poured myself another mug of tea. I recalled how Bryan had dealt with the boys graduating from riding tricycles to bicycles. Santa had given Meg a two-wheeler the year before we moved to the suburbs, and a couple of years later, Bryan and I felt it was time to upgrade the boys' wheels as well.

"If we could find used bikes," Bryan said, "I could fix them."

"Friday is the start of the city's white elephant weekend," I told him. One weekend every spring, the public works department encouraged residents to put unused items at curbside. People drove around the city to pick up items they wanted.

"That's a good idea, Val. I'll go out Friday after work and pick up as many bikes as I can. If I get four good frames, I can take wheels and seats from others and combine them."

Bryan had read about a way to teach children to ride a bike, without using training wheels. Two weeks later, after we had four bicycles in working order, he tested this theory.

He lowered the seats, and had each boy, one at a time, sit and move the bike with his feet. Once the boy felt comfortable doing that, Bryan held the back of the seat while the rider pedaled the wheels. After a day or two of doing this, the boy was able to balance on his own. Bryan released his grip on the bike for progressively longer periods, until the boy was riding on his own.

Watching him teach the boys to ride, I remembered that when we were dating, he had helped me get back on a two-wheeler. Living with my parents in my early 20's, I had bought an adult-sized tricycle. But I detested it. I felt it emphasized my disabilities, which I tried to pretend didn't exist. I refused to take it with me when I moved to Bala, the year I met Bryan.

He enjoyed riding his ten-speed, and he wanted me to join him. Not only did I not have a bike, I had to confess, I wasn't sure I could ride one. Bryan wanted me to try, and he refused to accept my lame excuses for not doing so.

We borrowed a bike in my size from a friend's sister. I discovered that riding a bike really is…like riding a bike. With Bryan holding the back of the seat, I dared to get on. I was very surprised and quite pleased to discover that after a few minutes he was running beside me with his arms at his side. I was riding alone! In celebration, he bought me my own three-speed bicycle.

Using this method of instruction again in 1991, it was only a couple of weeks until all four boys were able to ride by themselves. They rode in front of the house at first, but as they became more proficient, they went for longer rides. By the time he was in high school, Alan liked to ride his bike to school occasionally instead of taking the bus.

I finished my lunch, and it was time to switch the laundry. As I transferred the clothes to the dryer, I saw jeans for Geoff, track pants for Paul and Alan and cotton pants for Richard.

They had dissimilar tastes in clothing. They also wanted to do different extra-curricular activities. Paul took karate lessons at a dojo in the city. However, he was upset because Richard, who went bowling with Dad two or three times a month, could talk to him during the game, while he was unable to do so during his lesson. We could please some of our kids some of the time, but we couldn't please everyone all the time.

After we'd moved, one of our neighbours had given each of our sons a fifteen-minute weekly piano lesson. Alan had shown the most aptitude and interest, and the next year, he was the only one who took lessons. In return for the lessons, Bryan taught our neighbour and his wife how to use a computer. It was a fair exchange. Bryan accompanied Alan to his lesson, and then he stayed for an extra half hour to share his computer knowledge.

Geoff joined Meg in taking archery lessons for several years. After his interest in that waned, he developed a fascination with magic. He explored that on his own for a few months, reading books and practicing sleight of hand tricks. As he lost interest in that, and became proficient at reading, he spent all his spare time with a sci-fi book in hand.

Richard informed me that a boy could never have too much Lego. He used some of his paper route money to buy increasingly complex packages of the toy. He would build a Lego house for his sister, the year she left home to attend university, and give it to her for her birthday.

"Here, Meg, I made this so you could have a house of your own."

"Thanks, Richard. It's a little small though!"

It was small, but it had many other features she liked, such as the attached garage and multiple entrances. It had a garage door, regular door, and a roof top door.

I ceased my reminiscing, finished the laundry and returned to the kitchen. As I washed a couple of apples, and pulled a couple of bananas off the bunch sitting on the counter, I thought ahead a couple of days.

I still went to church regularly. I had taken the kids to Sunday school, but the year she turned ten, Meg had become an altar server. Three years later, the boys did as well. When the kids became servers at the church, Bryan's time at home alone ended. Only the children who were on duty went to church. I was happy to be the driver every week.

I had to stop thinking in the past, and continue getting snacks ready. The kids were always hungry the minute they got off the bus, and it made my life easier to have fruit, cheese and crackers on the table. Some days, I have to admit, Meg and I ate my carefully prepared snack while the boys went to the cereal cupboard.

As I watched the kids eating, talking and laughing among themselves, I was glad we had moved. This house had a bright airy feel to it that had been lacking in the other, older home. Yes, we were enjoying our house in the suburbs.

My term as an integral part of my children's growing up years was at an end. The children had come en masse, had gone through the various stages as one, and were maturing in a group.

Bryan and I found our function changing, but we tried to maintain our 50/50 rule. Besides positive and negative interaction, it now included taking time to find each child's forte and to fan that flame.

A new house...different parental roles...the children in school...our life was changing. But bigger changes were coming. Straight ahead were secondary school, the teen years, and driver's licenses. Where had the time gone? But I wasn't going to let myself suffer empty-nest syndrome, remember?

20: Transition

In June 1999, our sons graduated from grade eight. We had to buy four pairs of dress pants. Granny Jean, concerned that her grandsons look decent as they ended the first stage of their education, bought four white shirts. Bryan found four ties. They only had running shoes, though. We were loathe to buy four pairs of good shoes.

Richard and Geoff could wear shoes that Bryan no longer wore for work. His job allowed him to buy new shoes at a reduced price, every couple of years, and he took advantage of it. He was required to wear steel-toed shoes, but the two boys didn't mind wearing them for one evening. How to get shoes for Alan and Paul? I phoned my friend.

"Dawn, we need two pairs of dress shoes, for Alan and Paul to wear to their graduation next week. Does John have any extra?"

"I don't know, Val. I'll ask him and call back."

Dawn phoned later to say her husband had three pair, and they would drop by the next night after work. When they arrived with the shoes, I called Alan and Paul. They each found a pair they could wear.

It was a week before the graduation ceremony, and attire was assembled. Way to go, Mum!

That week, I found myself in a reflective frame of mind doing the housework. Sending the children to school had been my salvation. Our move to the suburbs coincided with our sons entering grade one. Should we separate the boys or put them in the same classroom? We consulted books, and talked to parents of twins, but the literature on this aspect of raising multiples didn't agree. Parents had differing ideas too.

We discussed the pros and cons of each scenario, but in the end, the situation resolved itself, at least partly, by the fact that we had enrolled Meg in the Roman Catholic School system.

Bryan is nominally RC and had gone through that system. I had gone through the public school system, but if Bryan wanted our children to attend RC schools, that was fine by me. I took them to the Anglican Church giving them exposure to that faith as well.

Further resolution came from the fact that we had put Meg in French Immersion. We both felt it was important to start learning a second language at an early age. There was only one French Immersion, Separate school for our kids to attend.

When the boys entered grade one, we had been given the choice of pairing our sons since there were two classes. Using GARP as a guide, I suggested Geoffrey and Alan to go into one class, and Richard and Paul into the other. The school had two classrooms of grade two, and two of grade three, making it easy to decide on the pairing. The four initials can be paired three different ways.

Only one son had been tentative about going to school. I had feared that some of my kids would have been like me. For my first two years at school, I had not wanted to go because it meant leaving my mother. It wasn't his mother that my son wanted to be close to—it was his brother!

Alan insisted on sitting beside Geoff in class, even though I had asked the teacher to seat the two boys on opposite sides of the room. He needed that proximity to his brother for several weeks.

And Babies Make Seven

A couple of years after we moved, the kids' bus had stopped at our neighbour's driveway across the street, which I could see out the front window. One morning I noticed Geoff standing in the driveway at 7:35 a.m., fifteen minutes early. I went out.

"Geoff, you don't need to be out here yet." I picked up his backpack and grabbed his hand to take him across the street.

"Yes, I do," he cried, digging in his heels. "Otherwise Meg will be first, and I want to be."

"Oh for heaven's sake." I could not think of what else to say.

Competition was fierce among the boys. I wondered when Meg had been implicated. That morning, Geoff had waited by the door until it was time to leave. When I gave the signal, he dashed across the street.

The grade one teachers spoke to their pupils in French, and may not have known much English. One day, I'd overheard Paul, Alan and Richard discussing how they learn French from their teachers and their teachers learn English from them. I laughed when I heard Paul say, "I taught my teacher to say 'Hasta la vista, baby'."

I finished vacuuming, and put the vacuum cleaner away to clear space for the kids to rush in and hit the cereal cupboard. I tried to stay out of the way, but I was happy being ignored–it meant things were running smoothly. Occasionally, however, someone needed to be driven to the library, or a friend's house. Then Mum's skills were necessary.

A few days later, I went grocery shopping. Reaching for the foods needed to make lunches, I wondered if the boys' preferences would change as they went into secondary school. I knew I'd still be responsible for making the sandwiches.

Because I'd been in the habit of making Bryan's lunch, it had seemed only natural that when Meg started going to school I would make hers as well. A few years later, when the boys started taking lunches as well, I was very adept at the practice. In addition, our larger house in the suburbs had a small kitchen, and it was easier for me to make five lunches than to have my children scrabbling around, trying to make their own.

Would I still need to enforce my two morning routine rules? They had worked well during the elementary school years, most of the time. I recalled one time I hadn't stuck to the second rule, and it had actually been beneficial. Maybe it's true: some rules are meant to be broken.

One morning, when the boys were in grade two, Paul was halfheartedly getting ready for school, coughing and saying he didn't feel well. I decided to let him stay home since he had a doctor's appointment that afternoon.

When we arrived at the office, the nurse took one look at him, whisked him to a back room, and gave him a mask to help him breathe. I hadn't realized his asthma was bad. After the doctor's examination, I took my son to the hospital. He spent two nights there.

After that episode, I made sure I knew what to look for, and started Geoff or Paul on their puffers four times a day, at the first sign of a cough. I soon recognized a pre-asthma cough as opposed to a fake 'I-have-to-stay-home-from-school' cough. As the two boys grew, they learned to monitor their symptoms themselves, carrying their puffers with them to use as needed. When Geoff was in grade nine, he played the French horn and the exercise of doing so increased his lung capacity such that he has had no problems since. Paul wasn't as fortunate, but he has been able to keep his symptoms under control.

There were other glitches with my rules. One morning, that same year, I noticed an empty sandwich container on the counter after the kids had left for school. It struck me as being odd, but I put it away without a second thought.

That afternoon, Paul got off the bus and stomped into the house. He slammed his backpack on the floor and said, "Mum, I'm really hungry because you *forgot to send my lunch!*"

I turned to look at him. I could almost see steam rising from his ears he was so upset. I thought back to the empty sandwich container I'd seen on the counter. Aha!

"What did you do at lunch?" I asked.

"The teacher asked Alan to give me half his sandwich."

"That was good of Alan. Do you want a sandwich now?"

"Yes, please." Paul was trying not to cry, and the prospect of a peanut butter and honey sandwich as an afternoon snack had appeal.

A new school had been built in our neighbourhood the year the boys went into grade four. This gave Bryan and me the option of putting two boys into an English stream, to ensure they were in separate classrooms. Which was more important: learning a second language or having the brothers separated?

Bryan and I considered our choices, and decided we were unwilling to take two boys out of French Immersion. Neither of us had started speaking French until we were in high school, and by then it was too late to learn the sounds that are unique to the French language. In the same way, my father, a native of Holland, was never able to pronounce the "th" sound because he hadn't learned English until he was in high school. We left our sons in French Immersion even though it meant they were in the same classroom for several years.

I had joined the Parent Teacher Association at the new school that year, and I went to help at a book fair. When I arrived at the school, I immediately headed to the library. Another parent was already there. She showed me where to put the money, and where to put the slips of paper so we'd know which books had been sold.

"The lower classes were in this morning. This afternoon it'll be grades four to eight," my co-worker told me.

"Oh good. If it's Shelley's class, the boys will be here."

"Yes, I think her class will be the first one down."

Sure enough, my sons were part of the first group of students attending the fair. Their teacher led them in and gave them instructions in French. I didn't understand, but the students all seemed to know what was expected.

Paul came over to the table. "Hi Mum. I didn't know you'd be here."

"Oh yes. I get around! Are you going to buy a book?"

"Maybe." He started to leave, but his teacher came over and spoke to him.

"*Paul, est-ce que tu savais que ta mère serait ici?*"

"*Non, je ne le savais pas.*"

I didn't understood the conversation, and when he told me later what they'd said. I wondered why he hadn't known I'd be there. Hadn't he listened to my recital of the day's events, that morning?

"Hi, Shelley," I said, after my son had walked away. "Are you prepared for our hour long interview Thursday night?"

"Oh yes, can't wait." She said, rolling her eyes.

While driving home from the grocery store, I remembered that the parent-teacher interview had gone well. That particular teacher had taught all of our sons in grades four and five, and we'd had four hours of interview time with her over the two years.

And Babies Make Seven

At the house, I put the food away, although sometimes I wondered why I even bothered. Food was consumed so quickly I could almost have left the boxes and cans sitting on the counter!

Two days later, it was the day before the boys' graduation. I was doing laundry while watching the evening news. Bryan was lying on our bed, also watching TV. I sat on my side of the bed, with the laundry baskets on the floor. I picked towels out of one, and began folding. After I'd finished with them, I started on the boys' clothing.

My sister-in-law had chided me for doing that. "Why bother folding them?" She'd asked last time we'd talked on the phone.

As I paired socks and folding pants, I realized that I did it because it was something *I* could control. Once the garments were in tidy piles, I put them in the proper drawers. Then I felt good. If everything became jumbled later, as the kids rooted through them, looking for something specific, that was not my problem.

The next afternoon I went to the school to watch the boys be clapped out and I drove them home so they could get ready for the evening's festivities. Grade eight graduations were treated more formally than in my day, but I was prepared, having been through the procedure a few years earlier, with my daughter.

Meg assumed her big sister role, as the boys were getting ready to go out that evening. She provided a little gel to tame a brother's sticky-up hair. She forbade a brother to wear white socks.

"It just isn't done," she said.

She ensured each of her brothers had his shirt tucked in properly. However, Dad helped knot four ties.

As Bryan and I watched the proceedings, we were both happy and sad. We had survived yet another stage in our sons' lives.

Transition

The start of high school meant choosing courses in preparation for careers. Would the boys want to stay together? Would they opt for different programs? How would they handle going off in different directions?

Bryan and I knew our tenure as active participants in our sons' lives was approaching the end. Whatever choices the boys made, each was responsible for his own path. Bryan and I were happy to hand over the responsibility, but we were always available for a consultation.

21: Off They Go

In August 1999, I took Geoffrey, Alan, Richard and Paul to the high school they would be attending in another month, to check out the used clothing sale. There was a dress code at the school.

"Here Geoff, hold this up to see if it'll fit." I handed him a blue and white long sleeved top.

"I'm not going to wear that, Mum." He was trying to whisper, not wanting to hurt the feelings of the mother who was trying to sell it. But at the same time, he wanted me to know how much he disliked it.

"What *will* you wear?" We were in the school gymnasium, walking up and down the aisles between tables of clothing being sold by students no longer attending the school, or their parents.

"Here Al, will you wear this?" I handed him another long sleeved top.

He glanced at in disdain. "No, Mum, I won't." He didn't lower his voice, but he smiled at the young girl behind the table, trying to soften his negative response.

"What *will* you wear?" I asked again.

"Short sleeved T-shirts"

That's what all four of them wanted to wear. Short sleeved T-shirts. After buying six of them, I bought four long-sleeved tops to have on hand when the weather turned colder. Then I bought four pairs of pants. We left to go to the store downtown that sold new uniforms, where we bought two more pants, and a couple more T-shirts.

Off They Go

"Oh well," I thought to myself. "It's not like I'll have to do this every year." We hadn't had to buy new clothes every year for Meg.

The first Tuesday in September, I watched my sons eating breakfast, dressed in their school uniforms, and I wondered if they were excited. Although I appeared calm and unruffled, I was excited, reliving my own first days at high school

Having all five children in secondary school meant adding shower times to our morning routine. Choreographing five of them required a system of grace and finesse, as if I was conducting a symphony.

There were ground rules. Each person was allowed ten minutes in the bathroom. As well, my first morning routine rule had remained in effect: I would only prepare a sandwich and a drink. An adjunct of this was that if someone wanted a lunch other than what he or she usually took, it had to be determined the night before.

First up were the two boys who slept in the bedroom on the main floor. The clock radio came on at 6:45 a.m. The first boy stirred and sleepily made his way into the bathroom. When he finished, he called his brother. When I heard the clang to indicate the water had been turned off after the second shower, I woke the boys in the upstairs bedroom.

One boy had a shower, and called his brother. When he finished, he stuck his head in his sister's room to call her. Through these comings and goings in the shower, (I had them use an egg timer to keep the tempo) I was in the kitchen, doing my part in the morning's performance.

White bread, brown bread, meat, cheese, lettuce, mayo, peanut butter, jam… making sandwiches, I was.

Meanwhile, my children ambled into the kitchen to get their breakfast and prepare their snacks. My orchestral piece had no vocals. Five teens, stumbling around preparing and eating breakfast; pulling snacks from the cupboard; filling lunch bags until...someone looked at the clock.

"It's 7:45!"

A flurry of activity..."Where's my book?" "Where's my binder?" "Mum, have you seen my homework book?" "What did I do with...?"

I lifted piles of papers on the dining room table, and picked up books that were on the floor. "Is this it?" "Are you looking for this?" Appearing to help, even if I wasn't, was preferable to me sitting, sipping a mug of tea.

Hurry...hurry...don't be late...find books, grab coats and shoes...the bus won't wait... Five one-armed hugs and a final door slam was the crescendo of my symphony for that morning.

Meg was proud and happy to have her brothers accompanying her. I watched them through the window, walking around the corner and out of sight. What a transformation—from four howling babies and a three-year-old clamouring for attention to a group of five teenagers discussing computers or Nintendo.

When the kids arrived home from school at 3:00 p.m., they wanted to relax. Meg liked watching TV, but the boys preferred to play Nintendo or computer games. It took a month or two to agree on a scheme. The TV or computer could be on until dinner at 6 p.m., but then had to be turned off until everyone's homework was done. This worked well as it took into account the kids' needs for veg time, and our parental need to know that schoolwork was being done.

The routine didn't always run smoothly. If one boy didn't have homework, he felt he should be able to play a game, but that made it harder for those who did have homework to concentrate. I thought these days were over! Mary Poppins...where are you?

Off They Go

Parent-teacher interview nights changed as well when the kids were in higher grades. Bryan and I stood in lines, in the gymnasium or cafeteria, with the other parents, waiting to talk to each teacher.

Bryan stood in one teacher's queue and I in another. The first one to the head of the line called to the other, and we talked to that teacher for ten or twenty minutes, depending on how many of our children he or she taught. Then we moved to the next teacher, standing in line again. Twice a year we went for interviews, but by 2001 it was easier, since Meg graduated that year, and we had four fewer teachers to visit.

None of our children had scholastic problems, which meant we didn't need to go, but we liked making the connection. It gave us a boost to hear positive comments about our children, and many teachers were curious about our life with quadruplets.

Since our children had been going to school with the same kids over the years, we recognized many of the other parents also waiting. The only time we saw most of them was at the school, and we caught up on what was happening with them as we slowly drew closer to the teacher.

The problem of separating the boys, which had plagued us over the elementary school years, was resolved in high school. However, it was a good news/bad news situation. It was good the boys were in different classes, but the bad part was having ten or fifteen teachers to visit. We tried to get there as soon as the event started, and often stayed until closing time. I still found it tiring to stand for more than ten or fifteen minutes and often had to find a chair to sit on while Bryan took over line placement duties.

The boys' differing interests affected their choice of courses. Alan, Paul and Geoff took music in grade nine. The next year, Alan and Paul joined the junior band, with Paul playing the flute, and Alan the clarinet.

Their choices intrigued me—my mother had played the flute and my father the clarinet in a community band in the 1960s. Karma, maybe?

Figure 23: Val and Bryan dancing!

In December, we attended band concerts. When Al joined the Jazz Band a year later, we invited friends to attend a dance, with music provided by the band. Bryan and I didn't usually dance, and the one time we took to the floor, our friends took a picture. Such as unusual moment-- preserved for posterity.

Besides being in the band, Alan was still taking piano lessons. However, he had switched to a different teacher in 1995. The next year, Geoff decided he wanted to take piano lessons again, and Bryan took them both to the new teacher, Sheila. Each boy listened while the other had his lesson. They were at different levels of expertise, and had distinct musical tastes. Alan followed the Royal Conservatory of Music, but Geoff preferred ragtime and blues tunes.

When Meg decided she wanted singing lessons, the same teacher was able to accommodate her, and when Paul was interested in learning more about compositional theory, Sheila taught him as well. The four of them continued their various music lessons until each left for university.

However, while they were at school, any other groups the boys joined happened during class hours. For me, the kids left to catch the bus in the morning, and they came home on the bus in the afternoon. I didn't have the same involvement in their academic lives that I'd had previously as a member of the Parent Teacher Association.

This is not to say the secretaries at the school didn't get to know me. Many days I stopped in to drop off a forgotten lunch bag or book, if I was going out anyway. As well, each time someone stayed home with a cold or the flu, I had to phone the school. One March, I had a different person home each day for a two-week stretch.

Overall, however, the kids were healthy, and they liked going to school. It left me free to pursue my own interests. I undertook to edit the newsletter for the church, and I became involved with a local drug awareness group. This last effort was an attempt at making amends—the car crash I had been involved in was a result of drunk driving. Working on the newsletter was a way of repaying the parish community for the help they'd given my family. Other opportunities for payback presented themselves...

In November, the year my sons were in grade seven, my neighbour phoned, "Val, are you doing anything for a half hour at 8:30 a.m.? I have to take my son to nursery school, and I wondered if you'd mind coming over to stay with the twins."

"Oh sure, I can do that. What do you want me to do?"

"They'll have been fed, and will be in the playpen. If you come over I can show you where everything is."

I agreed to go over later. My neighbour's twins would be two in January, and trying to get all three boys into snowsuits for the ten-minute ride necessary to take her older son to nursery school each morning was too much.

That afternoon after I returned from grocery shopping, I put the food away and headed across the street. I knocked on my neighbour's door, not wanting to ring the doorbell and perhaps waken sleeping babies. My neighbour came to the door and invited me in.

"I've just put them to bed," she said in a soft voice. "Let's go into the kitchen."

"We can talk better here," she said in a normal voice. "The sound seems to carry up the stairs, so I always feel I have to whisper when I'm talking at the front door."

I laughed. "I remember what that's like. You never want to disturb a slumbering infant, that's for sure."

I was glad to help. What goes around comes around...I felt I was repaying the women who had helped me over the years.

In 2001, our sons turned sixteen. Bryan and I wanted them to get their drivers' licenses before leaving to attend university. Alan was as eager to drive as Meg had been. Rick was lukewarm to the idea, and Geoff and Paul did not seem eager at all. I was surprised. I thought our sons would be as keen to drive as their dad was.

We'd enrolled Meg in Young Driver's to ensure that she learned to drive correctly without picking up bad habits. Naturally, the boys wanted to take the same course. We didn't get a group discount, but we did arrange a deferred payment plan that was easier on our pocketbook.

I refused to drive with anyone until after they knew the rules of the road, and how to operate the car, or in our case, the van. I knew what *I* had to do to drive, but I was not a teacher. Bryan was happy to assume the role of driving instructor. Once the kids had completed the first stage of getting their driver's license, I was willing to sit in the front seat with each of them.

Alan passed through the licensing procedure as quickly as he could. Richard took longer, but eventually had his license as well. The graduated part of the procedure meant that the person had five years to take the three tests and be qualified to drive. Geoff and Paul were almost to the fifth year, and in university, before they took their final test, but they both passed. I was glad to have five other drivers in the house as it relieved me of many driving duties.

June 2003 was final exam time—the last high school exams our sons would write. It was also time to get their school uniforms ready to sell. I retrieved the long-sleeved tops, the ones I'd bought four years ago in case they had needed something to wear in the colder weather. They had never been worn.

"Ah well," I thought. "At least they're good enough to sell."

Then I reconsidered. How much money would I earn selling the used uniforms? Would it be worth the effort of going to the school for an afternoon in August, at a time when we'd be driving the kids to universities?

"No," I thought. "I'll gather all the uniforms and give them to the school. They can give them to students who need them." It was another way to pass on the generosity we had received over the years.

And Babies Make Seven

Bryan and I were pleased our children were moving on, but it was also a melancholy time. All those years ago, when our children had started their school careers, we had thought it would never be over. But here we were--Meg was away at university and the boys were almost finished grade twelve. Our future roles promised more change.

We were enjoying an evening at home. The boys were studying, two in their bedrooms, one in the family room, and one in the room in the basement.

"Bryan, do you remember that time Meg had eight friends over, and we fed thirteen kids without blinking an eye?"

"Yes, I think I do. Didn't we order pizza?"

"Yes, we did, but everyone was really hungry and there wasn't enough. I had to go through the fridge and pull out all the leftovers I could find, to feed everyone."

"That rings a bell. And didn't you make a salad?"

"Yes, I used most of the food in the fridge, and had to go shopping the next day. We were worried at the time that if the boys were as popular, we could have had thirty-six teens to feed."

"I'm glad it never came to that."

I was glad as well. The boys had never had a multitude of friends over. The four of them hadn't seemed to need friends in the same way Meg had. I wondered if it was a gender difference, or a function of them being multiples. Probably a little of both.

The boys graduated from high school, but without the razz-ma-tazz of my daughter's graduation. They seemed more interested in receiving replies to their university applications than in going to a grad dance. I was pleased--having to rent four tuxedos would've severely strained our budget.

Off They Go

One day in June, Richard went out to get the mail.

"Hurrah! A letter from Ottawa University! I wonder if I've been accepted." He ripped it open and I watched his eyes as he scanned the paper.

"Yes!" he said as he pumped his fist in the air.

"How many more universities do you have to hear from?" I asked.

"Just one, Waterloo. I've already heard from Dalhousie and I've been accepted there, too."

Alan entered the room. "Have you heard from Ottawa? Sweet. Maybe I'll hear from them, although I really want to go to Simon Fraser."

The boys had sent out applications a few months earlier. Bryan had urged them to try for at least one university that was out-of-province, and only Paul hadn't. But since everyone had applied to two universities in Ontario, we had eleven universities to hear from before final decisions could be made.

There had only been one complication. Alan's request to Simon Fraser University hadn't been processed properly, and by the time he discovered it, he didn't have time to submit another. Since he had also been accepted at Ottawa U., he opted to go there.

Richard had decided to attend that university as well, and although they were in the same residence, they were on different floors. At Christmas, Alan would apply to the University of British Columbia, and be accepted for enrollment in September 2004.

Geoff had chosen to attend Wilfred Laurier University, and in September 2003, we drove him to Waterloo. Meg had transferred from Carleton U. to Waterloo University in 2002, into an urban planning co-op program. The two of them visited back and forth frequently over the years. Geoff liked being with his "big sister," although she was several inches shorter than he.

Paul was the only one who stayed in Peterborough, living at home while attending Trent University. I tried to treat him like a boarder, so he would have an experience similar to his brothers' but old habits die hard. I often made meals for him, rather than letting him cook for himself. I was more than happy to let him do his own laundry, though.

With only one son at home that fall, my life changed. I did two loads of laundry a week, rather than doing that many every other day. I could go three, four, or five days without entering a grocery store. If a desire to tidy the house hit me, and I succumbed, the house stayed neat for several days.

Bryan and I resolved to redecorate the family room in December, painting the walls and installing pine wainscoting. No longer a place to do homework, play pool or table tennis, it was to be to a true family room, complete with wood stove and comfortable chairs.

Our Christmas celebration that year was an adult affair. Not only did the kids get up to open their Christmas stockings at a reasonable hour, but also we had let Meg fill them and put them on the beds before she went to bed. Bryan and I already had visions of sugarplums dancing in our heads when she acted as St. Nick.

The next year, Bryan and I would celebrate our 25th wedding anniversary. The children would be home for one last summer before becoming firmly entrenched in university life. It was an ideal time to take a holiday.

22: We are Outta Here!

"Look," I said, shoving the brochure across the table. "This is what our stateroom will be like."

"And we'll have a balcony?" Bryan asked, sipping his beer.

"Yes, I said we wanted an outside room with a balcony, even though it's more expensive." I paused to sample my wine.

It was a Friday, the end of the week, and now that we didn't have youngsters to look after, or teens to drive around, Bryan and I were relaxing.

I passed him another brochure, saying, "This is one of the dining rooms on the cruise ship."

We were planning an Alaskan cruise in June, to be able to spend the longest day of the year as far north as possible, even though our anniversary wasn't until September.

We could have driven to Alaska, but I'd heard vacationers on cruise ships were treated very well. *That* was what I wanted! No more, "Mum, I need help..." No more "Mum, can you...." No more "Mum, where's my..."

Bryan was happy to indulge me. He liked the idea of being on the water. In fact, if I could tolerate this vacation without becoming seasick, he had ideas for future holidays. I thought I'd be fine, since the ship was large and quite stable (Bryan assured me) and we would always be near the coast—we weren't crossing an ocean.

Our travel agent had found us a cruise that was less formal. We could eat where we wanted, and with whomever, or by ourselves in our room. Such an agenda met with my approval. I had reached my limit of schedules, and wanted a reprieve.

When the babies had first come home from the hospital, I'd had schedules for feeding, schedules for eating and schedules for sleeping. Then, as they grew, we devised schedules for computer use, schedules for playing Nintendo, and schedules for watching TV. We even had schedules to make sure homework was completed on time. Schedules, schedules, schedules! Twenty years of them, and even though I couldn't have functioned without them, enough was enough! Not living with one for a week would be bliss.

We had nine months to wait, but anticipation was part of the fun. Since we were technically leaving Canada, we had to ensure our passports were in order. Neither of us had been out of the country in years. We made plans to stay with Bryan's sister in Vancouver for a few days on either end of the cruise, which would last a week.

The next morning, Bryan and I were still reveling in our newfound parenting roles.

"It's just the two of us, almost like when we were first married," Bryan commented.

"You think?" I said, looking at him in disbelief. In some ways, I supposed, it was—we were often the only ones at home. But in other ways, it wasn't. Paul still lived here, although he was away during the day, and even some evenings. We had a dog as well as a cat, whereas in the early years of our marriage we'd had two cats. Plus our other four children could show up at any time... But if Bryan wanted to think it was just like when we were first married, who was I to argue?

We are Outta Here!

"It has been fun, though, hasn't it?" I asked. "It was easier than going through five pregnancies."

"I don't think I could have survived you going through five pregnancies," my husband said, grinning. "But yes, it has been fun."

A month later, the three boys and Meg trekked home for Thanksgiving weekend. Going off to university had been the first time of separation for our sons. A month apart had been a start. Now they could spend a weekend together.

Bryan and I delighted in seeing every seat at the table filled. Conversation included the inevitable teasing and dreaded puns, as the four boys traded first year university stories. Meg filled in with what was coming in later years. After dinner, we gathered in the living room. Alan took his customary seat at the piano.

"I really miss Al's piano playing," said Bryan.

Meg and Granny Jean were enthusiastic in agreeing. My mother had recently moved to Peterborough. My father had died in 1999, as had Bryan's dad. His stepmother had died in 2002. Granny Jean was our offspring's only living grandparent.

After a visit, my mother returned to her apartment. I cleaned the kitchen (Bryan had cooked the turkey dinner, as usual) and he and I went to bed shortly after, giving the kids had a chance to visit together without parental presence.

The next day, we said good-bye to the four children who were returning to university. Alan and Richard left on an early morning bus. Geoff and Meg travelled in the afternoon. The weekend visit had been fun for all, with only an undercurrent of sweet sorrow. Like baby birds who return to the nest one last time before flight, our kids had returned home before leaving to start their own lives. Unlike baby birds, who never return to the nest, we knew our kids would be back, but the parent-child relationship had changed forever.

The next day, after Bryan left for work, I considered my options: What was the likelihood the kids would notice if I did not change the beds? No one else would be sleeping in them, until the kids came home at Christmas, when they would likely sleep in the same beds.

As I considered whether to remove sheets or not, it brought to mind another attempt at scheduling—we had gone from having four cribs and two beds to having six beds in the time it took to disassemble the cribs. As stated earlier, I needed time to adjust to change. I had been panic-stricken at the thought of having to change six sets of sheets in one day.

I had tried to work out a sheet-changing schedule, but failed. Putting fresh sheets on beds was not the most exciting aspect of family life, as evidenced by the fact that I was the only one concerned about it. But, if sheets had never been changed and there'd been complaints, it would've been my fault, I was sure of that. Although my efforts in that regard remained hit or miss over the years, no one ever did complain. Maybe Bryan and I had passed on our weak cleanliness genes to our kids!

Bryan's gene was even weaker than mine, but he knew I became distressed if the house remained messy for too long, and he co-opted the kids' help, as youngsters, to pick up toys.

"I want everyone to pick up three toys," he'd say. The kids would disagree about whether one wooden block counted as one toy, or whether two or three blocks did, but they discussed it with Bryan as they did the work. If there were more than fifteen toys lying about, he'd ask them each to pick up two or three more. That ploy worked for him, but when I tried it, my approach was wrong…

We are Outta Here!

"I want everyone to pick up three toys."

"Is this a toy?" One of my sons held up a wooden block.

"I don't know. Just do it…"

I didn't like having discussions with my children. After they started school, they could talk circles around me. It was easier to do the work myself than to try to enlist their help.

By their teenage years, though, I had reconsidered, and tried to broach the subject of them doing chores by recording each household task I did. My plan was to show them the list, at which point each would clamour to be given a job, to lighten my load. As with the 3 C's, however, it failed before lift off. Bryan and I believed in a democratic approach to parenting but there had been times when I had longed to be a tyrant.

My husband and I accepted the fact that we had different ways of dealing with our children, due in part to our different personalities. The limitations caused by my brain injury were also partly to blame.

Keeping in touch with them electronically was much easier than face-to-face encounters! We did that for two months, and by mid-December, the kids started arriving home for Christmas. Bryan had his usual two weeks off work, but we didn't have to rush out to buy presents as we'd done in earlier years. Instead, we were able to stay home and visit.

Bryan's aunts had sent money again, and we used it to go to the cinema. A new "Lord of the Rings" movie had just come out and we all wanted to see it. We adopted going to see a LOTR movie as a family tradition for several years.

Another tradition was attending the Christmas Eve service. When our teenage kids had been servers, Bryan had attended the December 24 service, to see the five children, helping at the front of the church. That

244

And Babies Make Seven

first Christmas after being away at University, our children were welcomed back into the server's ranks. Bryan and I attended with them.

As a family, we liked having traditions. We had instigated two at the boys' first birthday in 1986. The first involved the photographer at our local paper taking a picture of the children. Every August thereafter, he phoned to arrange taking two pictures—one of the kids and one of our family. He never charged for his services, and we discovered why, many years later.

On the day of the boys' birth in 1985, he had driven from Peterborough into the hospital in Toronto. Unfortunately, he had arrived after the designated time and had been told that he wouldn't be able to take any photographs. Bryan had been at the NICU at the time, and he had convinced the hospital staff to give him access.

The other tradition concerned Meg. Even though the giant white rabbit had not been a big hit, the idea of our daughter celebrating her anniversary of becoming a big sister every August 27 persisted. Each year, our friends asked her how she wanted to celebrate the anniversary, and over the years, she's done many different things, including going to a couple of musicals in Toronto and being taken out for dinners to restaurants of her choice.

A cherished memory is my six- year-old daughter walking up the street beside Dawn, with John following them, holding the train of Meg's make-believe formal gown. That time they cooked a special meal for her at their house. Another celebration memory is four university students dressed as rockers, lip-syncing a hit song, for my eight-year-old daughter and her five-year-old brothers.

After the New Year arrived, (we had spent its advent quietly; the kids had gone out with friends) Bryan and I settled once again into our quieter life. We kept in touch with our children by phone and over the internet.

Meg was living with us for a semester, doing a work term in Peterborough. I was busy planning our trip, with our travel agent's help, but checking any major decisions with Bryan.

Our plans had expanded to include more than just a cruise from Vancouver to Alaska and back. My brother and sister-in-law had suggested we stop over in Calgary to visit with them.

I told Bryan what they had suggested, and added, "If we're going to spend a few days in Calgary anyway, why not take the train to Vancouver?"

"Yes, that's a good idea. I've never taken a daytime train through the Rockies. There's a special tour you can take–The Rocky Mountaineer."

The next day I went to the travel agency to inquire about the possibility of taking that train. There were two classes–red leaf and gold leaf, with the latter being more expensive. She wrote the prices on a piece of paper so I could discuss them with Bryan. That night after dinner, I showed him the piece of paper.

"If we're going to do this, we may as well go first-class," said Bryan. "There's no point in spending a lot of money and then not being able to take pictures."

Bryan had bought himself a new camera and some special lenses. Photography was his hobby now he no longer had to help with childcare. He said he wanted a change from working on cars, and taking pictures of the kids had sparked a new interest.

When he suggested going first-class, I agreed and then added, "No wonder we don't have savings. As soon as one of us suggests spending money the other immediately agrees."

246

"Yes," said Bryan, smiling. "And your problem with that is…?"

"No, no," I said quickly. "No problem!"

We both laughed.

I continued to organize our trip, along with doing housework and my volunteer work. The university year ended in May and our sons returned home. Meg moved back to Waterloo, to attend classes. This time, however, instead of having four children at home, we had four young men, three of whom had been living on their own for eight months.

Bryan was glad to see them because he enjoyed taking long walks with one or two of them at a time, and discussing technology, space exploration, and philosophy. I was glad to have them home too, but for different reasons. I liked to know how they were getting on and what they were doing.

However, we were both glad to have them home while we were holidaying so they could take care of our dog. He had to take seven pills over the course of a day, and the kids knew how to force them down his throat.

The dog had developed heart problems in 2001, and had only been expected to live for three or four months. We'd put him on medication to control his symptoms, but three years later, he was still going strong. Our sons took good care of him while we were away. We were glad to have a few more months with our dog; he died that fall.

The day of our departure in June arrived. We travelled to the airport in a limo service, and flew to Calgary. After spending three days with my brother and sister-in-law, we boarded the train for the two-day trip to Vancouver.

Bryan's sister and brother-in-law met us and drove us to their house, south of the city. After visiting for a couple of days, our brother-in-law dropped us off in the underground garage, and we started the process of registering for our cruise.

We walked to the back of the queue, and as we inched our way along my excitement increased. This was amazing! No children to worry about. No head swiveling to keep my eyes on little kids while silently counting to five. This was quite unlike the vigilance required when taking four toddlers to the mall. That had called for constant counting to ensure we had ours, and only ours, with us. This was bliss!

We were heading off on an adventure, but this one was quite unlike the one we had been on for the past twenty years. It seems a good place to end my story.

We'd had twenty years of mostly good memories. I could, upon reflection, recapture the feeling of incredible amazement I'd felt in 1985 after hearing the results of the ultrasound. The absolute anger and frustration, the darkness that had descended before the boys entered school, was gone. However, I couldn't deny that it had happened.

Our sons, now fully-grown, were still similar but different. They had all gone to university, but had studied different programs.

I had an easy, comfortable relationship with all my children. It was no different with my son who had spent extra time in the hospital. As well, there had been no discernable differences over the years, because I'd breastfed my daughter, but hadn't done so with my sons.

Raising five children on my husband's salary did not differ drastically from my childhood, when my parents had had to raise three teens on a preacher's stipend. I was used to being a judicious steward of whatever funds were available, and Bryan and I liked going to garage sales. They had been a good source for children's toys.

And Babies Make Seven

This holiday with my husband, in anticipation of twenty-five years of married life, was going to be worry-free. I held onto Bryan's arm when I wanted to gaze around so I wouldn't have to worry about throwing myself off balance and having people wonder why I was drunk. No, wrong attitude! Who would care if I were? This was *my* holiday, and I was going to enjoy it, without worrying about…anything.

Then I remembered Bryan's response to people who, when meeting us for the first time, and being told we had five children, four of whom were three years younger than the first, had said we were 'brave.'

"Bravery involves choice," he'd scoffed. "And we didn't have any. Sometimes you just gotta do what you gotta do."

"That's true," I mused as we drew closer to the check-in counter. "That was also true all those years ago. I didn't choose to survive that car crash. When I woke up in a hospital bed and discovered I was still alive, I merely did what I had to do.

"Bryan is certainly right about our life. I did not choose to have four babies at once. After finding ourselves in that situation, Bryan and I simply did what we had to do."

This would be a terrific vacation—no children, nothing we had to do…just ourselves and a chance to do what *we* wanted. It had taken just two minutes to get to seven in 1985, but twenty years to get back to two!

Information can be obtained at www.ICGtesting.com
in the USA
1645050116

BV00026B/16/P